edTPA® Prep Book

By: Preparing Teachers

This page is intentionally left blank.

Written by Preparing Teachers

Printed in the United States of America

ISBN- 978-1-64768-471-6

This page is intentionally left blank.

Free Online Email Tutoring Services

All preparation guides purchased directly from Preparing Teachers includes a free four months email tutoring subscription. Any resale of preparation guides does not qualify for a free email tutoring subscription.

What is Email Tutoring?

Email Tutoring allows buyers to send questions to tutors via email. Buyers can send any questions regarding the exam processes, assessment handbooks, lesson plan ideas, clarification on commentary prompts, or the guide.

Preparing Teachers reserves the right not to answer questions with or without reason(s).

How to use Email Tutoring?

Buyers need to send an email to onlinepreparationservices@gmail.com requesting email tutoring services. Buyers may be required to confirm the email address used to purchase the preparation guide or additional information prior to using email tutoring. Once email tutoring subscription is confirmed, buyers will be provided an email address to send questions to. The four months period will start the day the subscription is confirmed.

Any misuse of email tutoring services will result in termination of services. Preparing Teachers reserves the right to terminate email tutoring subscription at anytime with or without notice.

Comments and Suggestions

All comments and suggestions for improvements for the study guide and email tutoring services can be sent to onlinepreparationservices@gmail.com.

This page is intentionally left blank.

Table of Content

Chapter 1 - Introduction to edTPA®..1

    What is edTPA®?...1

    What are the edTPA® areas?..1

    Overview of edTPA®...2

    What States are participating in the edTPA®?...2

Chapter 2 - How To Use This Guide?...3

    What is the purpose of the edTPA® Simplified guide?...3

    How is this guide organized?..3

    How to use the edTPA® Handbooks?..3

    Understanding edTPA® Glossary..4

Chapter 3 - Planning for Instruction and Assessment...5

    Overview of Task 1: Planning for Instruction and Assessment...5

    Context for Learning...5

    Lesson Plans...6

    Instructional Materials...6

    Assessments...7

    Planning Commentary...7

Chapter 4 - Instructing and Engaging Students...9

    Video Recording..9

    Common Video Recording Questions...10

    Instruction Commentary..11

Chapter 5 - Assessing Students' Learning...13

    Video or Audio – Evidence of Learning...13

    Observation Notes...13

    Student Work Sample Papers...14

    Evidence of Feedback...14

    Evaluation Criteria..14

    Assessment Commentary...14

Chapter 6 - Brainstorming Ideas - Getting Started..15

    Central Focus and Associated Lesson Plans..15

Early Childhood edTPA® Central Focus and Lesson Plans 15

Secondary History/Social Studies edTPA® Central Focus and Lesson Plans 16

K-12 Performing Arts edTPA® Central Focus and Lesson Plans 17

Chapter 7 - Developing edTPA® Lesson Plans 19

Starting edTPA® Lesson Plans 19

Key Sections to Include in Lesson Plans 20

Best Practices and Mistakes Made by Candidates 20

Chapter 8 - Assessments 23

Formal vs. Informal Assessments 23

Quantitative vs. Qualitative Assessment 24

Formative vs. Summative Evaluation 24

Standardized vs. Non-standardized Assessment 24

Norm-Referenced vs. Criterion-Referenced Assessment 24

Objective vs. Subjective Assessment 25

Constructing Assessments 25

Types of Test Questions 25

Validity and Reliability 26

Chapter 9 - Learning Theories 27

Behaviorism 27

Cognitivism 27

Constructivism 27

Connectivism 28

Social Learning Theory 28

Multiple Intelligences 28

Discovery Learning and Scaffolding 28

Learning Through Experience 28

Hierarchy of Needs 28

Stages of Cognitive Development 29

Spiral Curriculum 29

Differentiated Instruction 29

Chapter 10 - Communication and Academic Language 31

Receptive and Expressive Language 31

Language Function and Language Demands 31

edTPA® Requirement of Academic Language 33

Chapter 11 - Explanation of Planning Commentary 35

Central Focus 35

Knowledge of Students to Inform Teaching 36

Supporting Students' Learning 36

Supporting Development Through Language 37

Monitoring Student Learning 38

Chapter 12 - Explanation of Instruction Commentary 39

Prompting a Positive Learning Environment 39

Engaging Students in Learning 39

Deepening Student Learning During Instruction 40

Analyzing Teaching 40

Chapter 13 - Explanation of Assessment Commentary 41

Analyzing Student Learning 41

Feedback to Guide Further Learner 42

Evidence of Language Understanding and Use 42

Using Assessment to Inform Instruction 43

Chapter 14 - Special Education edTPA® 45

Assessments/Baseline Data 46

edTPA® Example and Reference Note 46

Task 1: Part A – Context for Learning Information 47

Task 1: Part B – Lesson Plans for Learning Segment 48

Task 1: Part C – Instructional Material 61

Task 1: Part D – Assessments and/or Data Collection Procedures 64

Task 1: Part E – Planning Commentary 70

Task 2: Part A – Video Clips 77

Task 2: Part B – Instruction Commentary 78

Task 3: Part A – Work Sample 84

Task 3: Part B – Completed Daily Assessment Records and Baseline Data 87

Task 3: Part C – Evidence of Feedback 93

Task 4: Part D – Assessment Commentary 96

Special Education Score and Evaluation Analysis 100

Chapter 15 - Elementary Education Literacy edTPA® 103

edTPA® Example and Reference Note 103

Task 1 Part A – Elementary Literacy Context for Learning Information 104

About the Class Featured for the edTPA® 104

About the Students In the Classroom 104

Task 1 – Part B – Lesson Plans for Learning Segment 106

Task 1: Part C – Instructional Material 118

Task 1: Part D – Literacy Assessments 134

Task 1 Part E: Planning Commentary 142

Task 2 Part A: Video Recording 149

Task 3 Part A: Student Work Sample 154

Task 3: Part B – Evidence of Feedback 161

Task 3: Part D – Evaluation Criteria 175

Elementary Education – Literacy Score and Evaluation Analysis 176

Chapter 16 – Lesson Plan Template 179

Chapter 1 - Introduction to edTPA®

What is edTPA®?

edTPA® is an assessment created by the Stanford Center for Assessment, Learning, and Equity (SCALE) and American Association of Colleges for Teacher Education (AACTE) organizations. The assessment is nationally distributed and scored by Pearson Education. edTPA® is designed to measure the readiness of entry-level teachers on key aspects of education: planning, instructing, and assessing. The performance-based assessment is a unique way for individuals to be exposed to teaching methods and tools prior to entering as certified full-time teachers. The assessment allows institutions to qualify the candidates' competences in teaching specific subject areas.

What are the edTPA® areas?

The following are the edTPA® areas available for students to complete:

- Agricultural Education
- Business Education
- Classical Languages
- Early Childhood
- Educational Technology Specialist
- Elementary Education (contains both Literacy and Mathematics components)
- Elementary Literacy
- Elementary Mathematics
- English as an Additional Language
- Family and Consumer Sciences
- Health Education
- K–12 Performing Arts
- Library Specialist
- Literacy Specialist
- Middle Childhood English-Language Arts
- Middle Childhood History/Social Studies
- Middle Childhood Mathematics
- Middle Childhood Science
- Physical Education
- Secondary English-Language Arts
- Secondary History/Social Studies
- Secondary Mathematics
- Secondary Science
- Special Education
- Technology and Engineering Education
- Visual Arts
- World Language

Overview of edTPA®

The edTPA® includes three main areas: planning, instructing, and assessing. In completing the edTPA®, the candidates are required to compile a portfolio, which includes lesson plans, student work samples, assessment tools, video recording, and commentary responses.

Planning for Instruction and Assessment Task – This section requires the candidates to develop 3-5 consecutive lesson plans along with providing associated instructional materials and assessments.

Instructing and Engaging Children in Learning – This section requires the candidates to record a video showing instruction of the lesson plans developed.

Assessing Children's Learning – This section requires the candidates to utilize assessment tools to show evidence of feedback along with students' progression toward the objectives of the lessons.

What States are participating in the edTPA®?

edTPA® has been accepted by many States and institutions. In fact, some States have made the teacher performance assessment a requirement by State law. The following is the list of States involved in the edTPA®:

Alabama	Indiana	Pennsylvania
Arizona	Iowa*	Rhode Island
Arkansas	Maryland	South Carolina
California*	Michigan	Tennessee*
Colorado	Minnesota*	Texas
Connecticut	Nebraska	Vermont
Delaware*	New Jersey	Virginia
District of Columbia	New York*	Washington*
Florida	North Carolina	West Virginia
Georgia*	North Dakota	Wisconsin*
Hawaii*	Ohio	Wyoming
Idaho	Oklahoma	
Illinois*	Oregon*	

NOTE:

The asterisk indicates the policy is in place for the State.

The above state participation data was obtained on January 1st, 2016

Chapter 2 - How To Use This Guide?

What is the purpose of the edTPA® Simplified guide?

The purpose of this guide is to provide a clear guidance to the candidates as they complete the edTPA® portfolio. This guide is written by individuals who have deep understanding of the edTPA® portfolios and processes. These individuals have supported many candidates in completing the edTPA® in various subject areas. This preparation guide contains the best practices, lessons learned, and common mistakes.

How is this guide organized?

The assessment handbooks provided by SCALE are filled with pages of excessive information. Students have indicated that the information in those resources is not well organized and confusing. This guide is to give clear and concise information in the following sequence:

- General information on planning, instruction, and assessment tasks along with the best practices and frequently asked questions.
- The guide provides a chapter on brainstorming ideas for the edTPA®. Having the right audience, approach, objectives, and lesson plan ideas are critical to ensure compliance with the edTPA® requirements. Starting the right way will prevent candidates from having to restart the process or struggle in the process of completing the edTPA® portfolio.
- Developing lesson plans is one of the most critical aspects of the edTPA® because they are the foundation of the portfolio. Having the right elements in the lesson plans can make the instruction and assessment parts a lot easier. The guide includes one full chapter on developing lesson plans aligned with the edTPA® rubrics.
- edTPA® requires the candidates to fulfill several video rubric requirements with a 15-20 minutes of video recording. This guide includes the best practices and what to include for the video submission to increase scores.
- The commentary questions in the assessment handbooks are not well explained, vague, and sound repetitive. This guide devotes three chapters to explaining exactly how to respond to the commentary questions.
- This guide includes one example of the Special Education edTPA® and one example of the Elementary Education Literacy edTPA®. The examples include lesson plans, instructional materials, assessments, commentary responses, feedbacks, student sample works, and video recording summaries. The edTPA® evaluation and scores are also included.

How to use the edTPA® Handbooks?

When reading this guide along with developing the edTPA®, having a copy of the assessment handbook is important. The publishers are not allowed to use the exact wording from the assessment handbooks due to copyright laws. This guide references the questions and/or summarizes the questions, so having the assessment handbook is useful.

Understanding edTPA® Glossary

Each of the edTPA® handbooks includes a glossary section. The glossary section is important as the edTPA® uses technical terms in different manners and has introduced new technical terms. Having an understanding of the vocabulary words allows the candidates to better understand the edTPA® handbook. At this time, the candidates should review the glossary section of the handbook.

Chapter 3 - Planning for Instruction and Assessment

Overview of Task 1: Planning for Instruction and Assessment

Task 1: Planning for Instruction and Assessment focuses on the candidates' ability to develop lesson plans appropriate for the students and the content being taught. The task compels the candidates to think about the students' prior knowledge, assessment tools, language use, research, and theories in the early stages of planning instruction. This task allows the candidates to show and analyze curriculum, instruction, and assessment to support learners of different backgrounds and abilities to meet standards for the content. This chapter is broken down into five parts that are required for the Planning for Instruction and Assessment Task 1, which includes:

- Context for Learning
- Lesson Plans
- Instructional Materials
- Assessments
- Planning Commentary

Context for Learning

The Context for Learning is a three to four page document that gives the candidates the opportunity to provide background information on the school, classroom, and students. Having background information is critical to understand expectations, limitations, and methods used during instruction.

The Context for Learning gives the candidates an opportunity to express any requirements outside the edTPA® requirements that may impact lesson plans, instructional materials, and/or assessments. The intent is to document special requirements, limitations, and expectations that impact the planning, instructing, and assessing of the students for the edTPA® lesson plans. For example, some schools may have special requirements for the candidates to follow in the classroom, which impact most of the lessons, but the requirements do not impact the lessons for the edTPA®. As a result, there is no need to document those requirements, limitations, and expectations. Only document what directly impacts the lesson plans, instructional materials, and/or assessments for the edTPA®.

In the Context for Learning, the students with specific learning requirements need to be identified. The purpose is to identify those students along with the supports, accommodations, and modifications necessary for those students to be successful.

As the edTPA® grader reviews the portfolios, the background knowledge assists the grader in understanding the approach the candidates took in instructing and assessing the students.

Lesson Plans

edTPA® looks for three to five lesson plans (or, three to five hours of instruction, if teaching is within large time blocks). For most edTPA® subjects, the lesson plans concentrate on the idea of the central focus with exception to Special Education edTPA®, which concentrate on a learning goal.

At a minimum, the lesson plans need to include the following:

- State Content Standards and/or Common Core State Standards
- Learning objectives
- Formal and informal assessments
- Instructional strategies
- Detailed procedures to conduct lessons
- Instructional resources
- Activities within the lessons that allow teachers to analyze language demands

Most importantly, the lesson plans need to be connected with one another. Each successive lesson must incorporate information presented in the previous lesson.

One goal of the assessment part of the edTPA® is showing the students' ability to progress toward the central focus (or learning goal) throughout the lessons. Having the lessons connected and built upon one another, gives the candidates the opportunity to see students progression toward the central focus (or learning goal).

Instructional Materials

Key lesson plan materials need to be included in the instructional materials section. This includes materials that are obtained from third party resources and original materials developed. Including all the materials might not be possible with the page restrictions, so the candidates must determine which materials are necessary for the grader to view.

The following are suggestions and ideas to consider when compiling the instructional materials:

- For Power Point slides, the candidates can include six slides per page as opposed to one slide per page.
- For Power Point slides, the candidates should include slides that are only absolutely critical to instruction.
- If the candidates are using short stories or novels, they can include the front cover or only pages that are critical to the lesson(s).
- Worksheets serving as formal assessments do not need to be included in the instructional materials because they are not used to teach the lesson.
- If the candidates are using flashcards, the candidates does not need to include all the flashcards. The candidates can make a note on the bottom of the page indicating that only few of the flashcards are included.
- If the candidates are using objects as instructional material, candidates can take picture(s) of the objects to include in the instructional materials section.

- Candidates using the whiteboard or chalkboard, can take picture(s) of the whiteboard or chalkboard to include in the instructional materials part.
- Candidates should not be submitting edTPA® portfolios without instructional material, and the candidates should not be forcing themselves to find instructional materials to include. Candidates forcing to include materials or struggling to identify materials need to revisit their lesson plans to ensure meaningful instructional materials are included.

Assessments

Assessments are used to monitor and evaluate students' learning prior to, during, and after instruction. Many assessment methods and approaches exist, and the candidates need to consider the best path to assessing the students.

The following are suggestions to consider when developing assessment tools:

- Include both formal and informal assessments that are aligned with the central focus (or learning goal for Special Education edTPA®) and objectives.
- Assessments for the edTPA® need to show ability to track the students learning progression.
- Assessments need to provide meaningful feedback to the students along with providing support to the students for further learning.
- Assessments need to be designed to track the students' performance on the objectives.
- Create assessments that assess for content, skills, and language.
- Consider having final formal assessment that cover students' knowledge on all the lessons to see if the students meet the objectives.
- edTPA® strongly encourages students' involvement in self learning and self assessing, so the candidates should develop assessment strategies and tools to involve students in the assessing process.
- Consider students with disabilities, learning needs, or English learners when developing assessments. One of the commentary questions requires the candidates to explain how their assessments are tailored for students with disabilities, learning needs, or English learners.

Planning Commentary

The planning commentary consists of a series of questions related to the lesson plans, instructional materials, and assessment tools developed. The key to answering commentary questions is to answer them clearly and directly; purposefully making long responses is not the approach to take.

Knowing some of the prompts of the planning commentary prior to developing the lesson plans and assessments can assist the candidates in developing appropriate lesson plans and assessments. This also makes writing responses to the commentary questions easier. Some of the topics covered in the planning commentary include:

- Identifying central focus (or learning goal), standards, and objectives.
- Explaining how the lesson plans are connected together.
- Explaining prior knowledge required to be successful during instruction.
- Connecting central focus (or learning goal) to community, personal, and cultural assets.

- Explaining how lessons, instructional strategies, and instructional materials are related to research and theory.
- Justifying instructional strategies and planned supports for the whole class, individuals, and students with disabilities.
- Describing language function, language demands, and language supports.
- Explaining how assessments provide direct evidence of the student learning.

For the planning commentary, the candidates need to write responses in the future tense as instruction has not been conducted.

Chapter 4 - Instructing and Engaging Students

Task 2: Instructing and Engaging Students focuses on having the candidates teach lessons to support and engage the students in learning. Task 2 aims at evaluating how the candidates provide a positive learning environment to engage in student learning, deepen student learning, use instructional strategies, and provide feedback. The task is broken down into two parts, which include:

- Video Recording
- Instruction Commentary

Video Recording

The first step prior to recording the lessons is to obtain permission to video record from students' parents or guardians. Many candidates question whether written permission is absolutely required. Obtaining permission is a requirement under the edTPA® guidelines and is also a good idea as the candidates will be recording children and teenagers. Schools may also require permission as the video(s) is/are going to a third party for grading purposes.

The edTPA® video that is submitted for grading needs to focus on:

- instructing the students on targeted learning objectives
- interacting with the students to deepen understanding
- facilitating the students interaction
- providing constructive feedback to the students

The following are additional suggestions and ideas for the video recording:

- Candidates and students need be heard loud and clear in the video. If the students are not heard loudly and clearly, the candidates can repeat the students' responses and questions. This will prevent the candidates from having to include transcripts of the video recording.
- Show respect and rapport to all learners and encourage respect among students.
- Instead of directly correcting the students, encourage or challenge the students to correct themselves or think deeper.
- Elicit responses, provide feedback, and give opportunities for the students to apply the feedback.
- If the students are not paying attention, make sure to address those students in a positive manner.

Common Video Recording Questions

Question 1 – I am student teaching and will not have the opportunity to teach again. Can I record everything and decide later which part to include for the edTPA®?

> Answer: Yes, the candidates can record instructing all lessons. The candidates should include the suggestions mentioned earlier throughout the video. Remember, the candidates can crop videos, but cannot edit videos.

Question 2 – What if some students gave me permission to video record and others did not?

> Answer: Candidates can blur students who have not given permission to be in the video.

Question 3 – What if I am not teaching and need to complete the edTPA®? What are my options for video recording?

> Answer: There are few options available for video recording when the candidates do not have access to a classroom. These options include:
>
> - Option 1: Ask a local school to video record by doing volunteer work.
> - Option 2: Explain the instructions of the lesson(s) on a video in the first person. Candidates need to get permission from the State to take this approach. Make sure to obtain written confirmation from the State that this is acceptable.
> - Option 3: Get one or several children (friends and/or relatives) and use them as the students for the learning segment. This approach has been widely used for the Special Education edTPA® as the candidates can do individual instruction with justification.

Question 4 – In my video, I show slides or write on the whiteboard, which are not clearly shown in the video. What are my options?

> Answer: The candidates can include the slides or pictures of the whiteboard in the instruction commentary as the candidates are allowed to include two additional pages to support documentation of video recording.

Question 5 – For the commentary, am I restricted to only write about the video recording submitted?

> Answer: Majority of the responses need to be related to the video with time references. However, the candidates can write about instructions not included in the video, but this should be minimal.

Instruction Commentary

The instruction commentary consists of a series of questions related to the lesson plans included in the video submitted for grading. The key to answering the commentary questions is to answer them clearly and directly; purposefully making long responses is not the approach to take.

Knowing some of the prompts of the instruction commentary prior to recording can assist the candidates in developing instruction aligned to the edTPA® requirements. This also makes writing responses to the commentary questions easier. Some of the topics covered in the instruction commentary include:

- Explaining how the candidates demonstrated mutual respect, rapport, and responsiveness.
- Explaining how the candidates challenged the students to engage in learning and to engage with other students.
- Explaining how the candidates elicited response from the students.
- Describing how the instruction is linked to students' prior academic learning and community assets.

This page is intentionally left blank.

Chapter 5 - Assessing Students' Learning

Task 3: Assessing Students' Learning focuses on using the assessment tools developed in Task 1 and analyzing students' performance in relation to needs and identified learning objectives. Assessing on the objectives of the lessons is the key element for the edTPA® otherwise there is no purposeful meaning to assessing.

Task 3: Assessing Students' Learning is broken down in the following parts:

- Video or Audio Evidence of Learning
- Observation Notes
- Student Work Samples
- Evidence of Feedback
- Evaluation Criteria
- Assessment Commentary

This chapter will focus on Assessing Students' Learning for all subject areas of edTPA®. Special Education will be discussed in more detail in a later chapter due to several different requirements.

For Task 3, the candidates are to select one common assessment from the learning segment for analysis purposes. The selected assessment needs to be meaningful and focused on the objectives and standards. The assessment can address the entire learning segment, or the assessment can be one that is focused on any one of the lessons of the learning segment. Depending on the edTPA® subject, the candidates need to identify 1-3 focus students, for whom the candidates need to collect documentation supporting evidences of learning. The focus students' common assessments that are used for evidence of learning are submitted as part of the edTPA® portfolio.

Video or Audio – Evidence of Learning

Depending on the edTPA® subject area, the candidates are to provide additional video/audio showing evidence of learning. The video/audio clips need to be evidence of the students learning the objectives (or development of language for Early Childhood edTPA®). The video clips must show the students learning and not the candidates instructing the entire time.

Observation Notes

For the Early Childhood edTPA®, the candidates are required to provide observation notes for the focus students. These are general notes about the students' progress and responses during the learning segment. The notes need to show the students' development of language and literacy skills.

Student Work Sample Papers

edTPA® portfolio requires the candidates to submit sample work of the students associated with the common assessment. This is a very easy part to complete as the candidates need to submit the students' work (without any feedback). If the common assessment selected is meaningful and addresses objectives and standards of the lesson, this part is easily completed. When submitting the documents, the names of the students need to be marked out; the candidates can replace names with Student 1, Student 2, Student 3, etc. One task requires submitting sample works without feedback and another task requires submitting sample works with feedback. The best approach is to make additional backup copies of the students' sample works in case mistakes are made when writing feedback.

Evidence of Feedback

Evidence of Feedback is a critical part of Task 3, and the evidence can be provided either with video(s)/audio(s) or sample works. When giving evidence of feedback via video(s)/audio(s), the clips must show the candidates providing the evidence to the focus students. Moreover, the feedback needs to be connected to the evaluation criteria (discussed next). Feedback must be given consistently (similar amounts to each student), and the feedback can to be positive and/or negative.

When giving feedback on work samples, the candidates need to make sure to provide both positive and/or negative feedback. Candidates should circle any mistakes on common assessments. Make sure the final grade is circled on the top of the paper.

Evaluation Criteria

Candidates are required to submit evaluation criteria associated with the common assessment. An example is a rubric that addresses various aspects of the common assessment. The evaluation criteria must be related to the central focus and objectives. The common assessment and associated evaluation criteria can be used to identify patterns of learning (both quantitative and qualitative).

Assessment Commentary

The assessment commentary consists of a series of questions related to the common assessment, learning, and evaluation criteria. The key to answering commentary questions is to answer them clearly and directly; purposefully writing long responses is not the approach to take.

Knowing some of the prompts of the assessment commentary prior to developing the assessment tools can assist the candidates in developing tools aligned with the edTPA® requirements. In addition, writing responses to the commentary questions will be easier. Some of the topics covered in the assessment commentary include:

- Learning objectives and standards associated with the common assessment
- Summary of students' learning on all evaluation criteria
- Details of how the feedback is related to focus students' developmental strengths and needs
- Details of how the candidates supported the students in applying feedback to guide improvement

Chapter 6 - Brainstorming Ideas - Getting Started

Getting started with the edTPA® can be frustrating with all the information in the handbook provided by SCALE. Most candidates have never attempted the edTPA® and are unsure of how to get started. Candidates ponder on how to incorporate complex approaches or novel teaching methods. Some wonder on including a lot of activities within the lesson plans to maximize score. With edTPA® being a subjective assessment and having no knowledge of the graders, the best approach is to keep it simple and comply with the requirements of the edTPA®.

This chapter covers the following:

- Central Focus and Associated Lesson Plans Ideas
- Early Childhood edTPA® Central Focus and Lesson Plans
- Secondary History/Social Studies edTPA® Central Focus and Lesson Plans
- K-12 Performing Arts edTPA® Central Focus and Lesson Plans

Central Focus and Associated Lesson Plans

The central focus is a statement of the most important and critical concepts that the candidates want the students to develop within the learning segment. The central focus is one statement that is associated to all of the lesson plans. A common mistake by many candidates is having a central focus for each of the lessons. Lesson plans within the learning segment must be connected to achieve the central focus. The central focus has to be aligned with the objectives and educational standards. Each edTPA® subject assessment has additional requirements for the central focus. Candidates need to reference the handbook to know exactly the additional requirements needed for the central focus.

Early Childhood edTPA® Central Focus and Lesson Plans

For the Early Childhood edTPA®, the candidates are required to have a central focus that allows active and multimodal nature of learning and age appropriate learning of language and literacy within an interdisciplinary context.

For more information on the active nature of young children's learning and the multimodal nature of young children's learning, see the glossary of Early Childhood edTPA® Handbook.

Example: Second Grade

Central Focus: Students are to gain knowledge of vocabulary words to support them in comprehending and comparing literature related to the field of history.

The following are the lesson plans associated with the central focus:

- Lesson 1: Students will be learning vocabulary words associated with the reading passages.
- Lesson 2: Students will read the first passage that contains vocabulary words from lesson one.
- Lesson 3: Students will read the second passage that contains vocabulary words from lesson one.

- Lesson 4: Students will compare the passages in lesson two and lesson three by recalling details and main ideas.

The central focus involves active learning as the students will be involved in reading, and the central focus involves multimodal nature of young students' learning as students will use multiple senses (listening and viewing). The passages along with the vocabulary words are grade appropriate. As indicated before, lesson plans need to be connected to each other and connected to the central focus. Lesson two and three are connected to lesson one, and lesson four is connected to the first three lessons.

Secondary History/Social Studies edTPA® Central Focus and Lesson Plans

For the Secondary History/Social Studies edTPA®, the candidates are required to have a central focus that allows:

- students to learn and use facts and concepts
- students to inquire, interpret, and analyze arguments/conclusion about historical events

For more information on the central focus for Secondary History/Social Studies edTPA®, see the glossary of Secondary History/Social Studies edTPA® Handbook.

Example: Eighth Grade

Central Focus: Analyze the lasting impact of the Declaration of Independence and the Article of Confederation. In particular, analyze the impact of the two documents on the United States Constitution.

Lesson 1: Students will be presented information on the Declaration of Independence and will read a portion of the Declaration of Independence. Students will summarize the information in their own words. Students will also be completing a worksheet to test knowledge presented in the lesson.

Lesson 2: Students will be presented information on the Articles of Confederation and will read a portion of the Article of Confederation. Students will summarize the information in their own words. Students will also be completing a worksheet to test students' knowledge presented in the lesson.

Lesson 3: Students will get together in groups and compare and contrast the impact of the Article of Confederation and the Declaration of Independence.

Lesson 4: Students will be taught a lesson regarding the United States Constitution and will read a portion of the United States Constitution. Students will analyze the impact of the Articles of Confederation and the Declaration of Independence on the United States Constitution.

The central focus involves learning the facts and concepts of the Articles of Confederation, the Declaration of Independence, and the United States Constitution. In addition, activities include analyzing primary sources, which involves interpretation and analysis of historical events. All lessons are connected to the central focus, and the lesson plans build on one another.

K-12 Performing Arts edTPA® Central Focus and Lesson Plans

For the K-12 Performing Arts edTPA®, the candidates are required to have a central focus that supports students in:

- creating, performing, or responding to music/dance/theater
- applying artistic skills, knowledge, and contextual understandings

For more information on central focus for K-12 Performing Arts edTPA®, see the glossary of K-12 Performing Arts edTPA® Handbook.

Example: Middle School Level

Central Focus: The students will be taught the blues by playing harmony, improvising over the harmony, and analyzing the impact of the blues on society.

Lesson 1: Students will gain an understanding of the blues harmony (I, IV, V) on their instruments and verbally. Students will also learn how to play the blues using single notes, triads, and the sixth note chords.

Lesson 2: Students will learn to sing and play the harmony of I, IV, V over the blues and will create simple melodies over the blues using the blues scale. Students will learn to improvise over the blues using triads and the blues scale.

Lesson 3: Students will compose new music using the harmony of I, IV, V creating their own harmonic patterns and forms.

The central focus allows the students the opportunity to understand the historical significance of the blues through class discussion. Composing/arranging music allows the students to show creativity by creating their own melody using notes from the blues' scale.

This page is intentionally left blank.

Chapter 7 - Developing edTPA® Lesson Plans

One of the main documents that the edTPA® graders look at first are the lesson plans. The lesson plans must show compliance to the edTPA® requirements. Lesson plans need to be written with details that will allow another teacher to instruct the lesson plans without having difficulty. This section will contain information to develop lesson plans that are aligned with the edTPA®. This chapter contains the following information:

- Starting edTPA® lesson plans
- Key sections to includes in the lesson plans
- Best practices and common mistakes

Starting edTPA® Lesson Plans

When starting the lesson plans, the activities and objectives need to be grade appropriate. This requirement is important to ensure the students are able to learn the materials being presented. This also ensures the students will have the necessary background knowledge to complete the activities of the lesson plans. Prior to developing the lesson plans, the candidates need to keep in perspective the students with disabilities, as they must also complete all the activities. In fact, identifying the focus students should be done in the early stages to ensure those students learning needs are taken into account during the development of the lesson plans.

Remember that the lesson plans need to be connected with one another. First, write down the lesson plan activities and associated objectives. Next, find academic standards that can be linked to the objectives. Having standards associated with each of the objectives is absolutely necessary. If standards cannot be found, revisit the lesson plan ideas. In the early stages of developing the lesson plan ideas, the candidates need to consider including activities that involve language function and language demands. Then, write the central focus statement, which needs to have some reflection of all the lesson plans.

Engagement and interaction are key aspects of the edTPA®. Candidates need to include activities that allow students to engage and interact in the learning process. Many ways exist to get the students to engage and interact, some include:

- Engaging with technology (Power Point slides) – It is best to have slides that are two-way presentations as opposed to one-way presentations.
- Empower students – Letting students know that the activities are important provides a sense of ownership. This empowers students to dig deeper and ask more questions.
- Encourage students to fail – Reward students for failing. Let them fail early and often. Having students fail, allows them to learn and remember.
- Let them find their own way – Giving students an opportunity to reach the answers independently allows them to expand their mindsets.
- Checking for understanding– Stopping instruction and asking questions can determine the effectiveness of the lesson plan.

- Arrange competition – By introducing competition into the learning process, students are more likely to pay more attention and work harder to be the winners.
- Group activities – Stopping instruction and having a short group activity can help with engagement and ensure learning.

Key Sections to Include in Lesson Plans

Many templates exist for lesson plans, and in addition, some schools/universities require certain templates and sections to be included in the lesson plans. Candidates need to include only relevant sections in the lesson plan. To have meaningful and relevant lesson plans, the following sections are highly recommended for the lesson plans:

- Lesson Title
- Grade Level
- Central Focus (this is the same statement for each lesson plan)
- Educational Standards
- Lesson Objectives
- Instructional Material/Resources (list of materials/resources)
- Technology Integration (if applicable)
- Identification of Students Prerequisite Knowledge and Skills
- Instructional Procedures (step by step instructional procedures)
- Closure Procedures
- Guided Practice/Independent Practice/Feedback Application/Learning Supports
- Differentiated Instruction (accommodating students with disabilities or English learners)
- Assessments (include description of each assessment – both formal and informal)

Best Practices and Mistakes Made by Candidates

The following are best practices and common mistakes made by the candidates in developing lesson plans:

- Candidates include many objectives associated with the lesson plans and many academic standards. Candidates want to include objectives and standards that are strongly related to the lesson plans. Some candidates include standards that are only discussed for several minutes during instruction, and this is not the best approach. Academic standards should be documented only if the standards are meaningfully instructed and assessed.
- Candidates develop assessments that are not related to the objectives of the lessons. All objectives in the lessons need to be assessed.
- Candidates provide too many unnecessary details in the lesson plans. The most detailed section of the lesson plan needs to be the instructional procedures.
- Candidates start addressing questions of the planning commentary in the lesson plans. For example, the students write about learning theories in lesson plans, but that is unnecessary. Or, the candidates write about how assessments are tailored to English learners or special education students.

- Referencing the instructional material in the lesson plans is a good idea as that makes the grading process easier.
- Candidates use templates with tables and/or pre-populated questions. These templates take away paper space and can increase the number of pages. If the lesson plans have a lot of white space, consider using an outline approach (see Chapter 16).

This page is intentionally left blank.

Chapter 8 - Assessments

The purpose of assessments is to guide instructional decisions throughout the learning cycle. Prior to teaching, assessments are used for planning instruction and subsequent assessments. During teaching, assessments are used to determine the effectiveness of instruction and used to modifying teaching methods. After teaching, assessments are used to determine if revisions are needed for future instruction and to understand the students' performances. Each of the tasks of edTPA® involves assessments in some way. Having knowledge of the type of assessments will help candidates determine which assessments to use in the learning process. This chapter covers the following:

- Formal vs. Informal Assessments
- Quantitative vs. Qualitative Assessments
- Formative vs. Summative Evaluations
- Standardized vs. Non-standardized Assessments
- Norm-Referenced vs. Criterion-Referenced Assessments
- Objective vs. Subjective Assessments
- Constructing Assessments
- Validity and Reliability

Formal vs. Informal Assessments

Formal assessments have data that measure how well students' perform on the learning outcomes. These assessments contain data for assessing overall performance, comparing students' performance with others, and identifying strengths and needs.

On the other hand, informal assessments, also known as criterion referenced assessments, are not data driven but rather performance driven and content driven. Running records are informal assessments; running records indicate how well a student is reading a book. Informal assessments support teachers in understanding the effectiveness during instruction.

Formal assessments are planned in advance and delivered at the end of instruction. Informal assessments are more spontaneous and occur during instruction. Below is a table with examples of informal and formal assessments.

Informal Assessments	Formal Assessments
- Pre-assessment - Checking for understanding - Questioning strategies - Observation checklists - Exit cards	- Tests/quizzes - Authentic assessments - Performance assessments - Portfolios - Projects - Lab reports - Word problems - Essays - Graded homework - Final exam

Quantitative vs. Qualitative Assessment

Quantitative assessments and qualitative assessments are needed for the edTPA®. Quantitative assessment methods yield numerical scores, which include teacher-constructed tests, standardized tests, checklists, and rating scales. Qualitative assessment methods include yield descriptions of characteristics, which include teacher observations, anecdotal records, and informal questions.

Formative vs. Summative Evaluation

Formative evaluation is a decision making process that occurs during instruction. This approach is taken to make necessary adjustments to the lessons to accommodate students' needs. Even though the students are being assessed, formative evaluation allows an evaluation of one's own teaching rather than the students' work. Formative evaluation can be based on formal or informal methods.

Summative evaluation happens at the end of instruction, which can be at the end of a chapter, unit, or semester. This approach is used for assigning grades, promoting students, or retaining students. Summative evaluation is solely based on formal assessment methods.

Standardized vs. Non-standardized Assessment

Standardized assessments are administered, scored, and interpreted in the same manner for all students and primarily used to compare students from different schools, States, etc. Non-standardized assessment methods are made by teachers for classroom use and are used to determine the extent to which subject matter is being taught. Non-standardized assessment methods are primarily used in the edTPA® portfolio.

Norm-Referenced vs. Criterion-Referenced Assessment

As indicated by the name, norm-referenced assessments provide information on where an individual student's performance is in relation to his or her peers. Usually, standardized tests are norm-referenced, and the results are quantitative. Criterion-referenced assessments compare students' performance to pre-determined objectives; Criterion-referenced assessments can be quantitative, qualitative, or both.

Objective vs. Subjective Assessment

Objective assessments are those assessments that do not determine scores based on judgments. These assessments contain only one correct answer, which can be multiple-choice, true-false, or matching items. Subjective assessment methods involve judgments. Subjective assessment methods may have several possible correct responses or a single correct response with several ways to arrive at that response. Examples of subjective assessments are short-answers, essay items, or constructed response.

Constructing Assessments

Constructing assessments need to be fair to ensure proper understanding of students' learning and performance. To construct effective and fair tests, the candidates need to have assessments that are related to the objectives of the lessons. The assessments need to reflect the knowledge and skills the students are taught and need to be proportional, meaning more points for more critical information. In addition, the types of test questions need to be fair for the students to show learning. Giving the students appropriate time to complete the test is also a factor of fair assessments.

Types of Test Questions

Various types of questions can be included on assessments. Understanding the options available will allow candidates to select appropriate questions for the edTPA®. The following are some common types of questions:

Essay – This requires more time for the students to complete. The prompt for the essay needs to be clearly stated.

True/False – This gives the students 50% chance of guessing correctly, so it is not the best assessment of their knowledge. For these questions, avoid using "always" and "never."

Multiple choice exam – This is a very efficient form of assessment. In developing multiple choice questions, avoid:

- Stem clues in which the same word appears in the stem and an option.
- Grammatical clues in which an article, verb, or pronoun eliminates options from being correct.
- Repeating the same words across options
- The use of "all of the above" (discourages discrimination) or "none of the above" (encourages guessing).

Recall Items – These are short answers and fill in the blanks, which require the students not also to recognize the answer, but to also write the answer in.

Matching items – These include two lists requiring students to match up items between them.

Validity and Reliability

Validity refers to whether a test measures what it says it measures, and this can be done by content validity, concurrent validity, and predictive validity. Content validity is established by examining a test's contents. Concurrent validity is correlating the scores on a new test with scores on an established test given to the same individuals. Predictive validity is by correlating the scores on a new test with some future behavior of the students that is illustrative of the test's content. Reliability is whether a test results in the same or similar scores consistently, and reliability can be confirmed by retaking the test or delivering the test in alternative forms.

Chapter 9 - Learning Theories

Each of the tasks of the edTPA® requires the candidates to reference learning theories and research. The purpose of this chapter is to provide information on common learning theories and research available to consider during planning, instructing, and assessing. The information presented here on the learning theories is at an high level as extensive details are associated with these theories/research. The candidates are recommended to conduct additional research to gain more understanding of the theories. The learning theories/research mentioned in this chapter are only a few of the many available for candidates to incorporate in the edTPA® portfolio.

Behaviorism

Behaviorism learning theory is the process of assessing and changing associations between stimuli and responses. Burrhus Frederic Skinner (B.F. Skinner) is well-known for the operant conditioning; learning process is due to changes in behavior. Operant conditioning is a controlled response with a reward or punishment dependent upon the behavior. Ivan Pavlov is known for the classical conditioning, which is an unconditioned stimulus and response that is manipulated with a conditioned stimulus to result in a conditioned response. The techniques of reinforcement and punishment are used in classrooms to encourage good behavior and eliminate bad behaviors.

Cognitivism

Cognitivism refers to information processing, and how individual minds obtain, processes, and stores information. In this theory, the mind functions as a computer processor with information being inputted into the mind, being processed, and being stored. Learning is achieved through repetition and consistent use of the information.

Constructivism

Constructivism involves individuals constructing their own knowledge, which is based on personal experiences and interactions with the outside world. Individuals consume new information and interpret it base on their attitudes, beliefs, and experiences. When constructivism is employed in the classroom, teachers encourage the students to explore within a given framework.

Lev Vygotsky is well-known for social constructivism, which states that the students learn and establish meaning to information via social interaction. Vygotsky is famous for the concept of Zone of Proximal Development, which states learners can gain knowledge independently to a certain level, but can increase knowledge by interacting with other classmates and instructors. Jean Piaget introduced cognitive constructivism, which states that knowledge is gained by either assimilation or accommodation. Assimilation is an ongoing process in which the students cognitively adapt and organize information by imploring current way of understanding to analyze experience and the outside world. Accommodation involvers thinking changes when new information is unable to fit into old ways of understanding.

Connectivism

Connectivism is a learning theory in which learners build knowledge in process of understanding experiences. Information changes quickly and exists outside of the learners. The learners establish connections between information to enhance knowledge, establishing an independent learning network.

Social Learning Theory

Albert Bandura is known for the social learning theory, which states that learning occurs in the social context via observation or direct instruction. Two versions of social learning theory exist: vicarious learning and pure modeling. Vicarious learning occurs when others get punished or rewarded in front of the learner. Pure modeling is when no one is rewarded or punished.

Multiple Intelligences

Howard Gardner is known for the Multiple Intelligences Theory, which states that each learner has the following measurable forms of intelligence: linguistic, logical-mathematical, spatial, body-kinesthetic, musical, intrapersonal, and interpersonal.

Discovery Learning and Scaffolding

Jerome Bruner is recognized for the discovery learning and scaffolding theory in which individuals create new ideas or concepts from previous knowledge or past experiences. Discovery learning teaching provides the students opportunity to discover new information independently.

Learning Through Experience

John Dewey's theory of learning through experience encourages open-minded activities and individuality, such as art-integration or cooperative learning.

Hierarchy of Needs

Abraham Maslow is known for his theory of hierarchy, which states that certain lower needs must be satisfied before higher needs can be achieved. The needs identified include:

- Self-actualization
- Esteem
- Love
- Safety
- Physiological

Hierarchy of Needs can be used in classroom environment to ensure that the needs of the students are being satisfied.

Stages of Cognitive Development

Jean Piaget is known for the four states of cognitive development:

- Sensorimotor (Birth to 2) – Explore the world through motor skills and senses
- Preoperational (age 2 – 7) – Believe others view the world as they desire
- Concrete operational (age 7 – 11) – Reason with logic
- Formal operational (11 and up) – Use abstract thought

Spiral Curriculum

Spiral curriculum is when learning is distributed over time rather than being condensed in shorter periods. Repetition over months and across grade levels is an indication of spiral curriculum.

Differentiated Instruction

Carol Ann Tomlinson is known for her research in differentiation, which is tailoring instruction to meet individual needs. Differentiation can be in content, processes, the learning environment, and assessments. Differentiation is a way for teachers to respond to students' learning needs.

This page is intentionally left blank.

Chapter 10 - Communication and Academic Language

Communication and academic language are important in the learning process. The two are ongoing in the classroom, and the edTPA® requires analysis of the two in the portfolio. In the context of the edTPA®, communication is how the candidates support the students in developing the ability and skills to be understood. Academic language is the formal language used in classrooms, found in textbooks, and presented on assessments. This chapter covers the following:

- Receptive and Expressive Language
- Language Function and Language Demands
- edTPA® Requirement of Academic Language

Receptive and Expressive Language

Receptive language is listening and understanding language and expressive language is the ability to communicate with others using language. Expressive language involves communicating while receptive language involves comprehending. Words that indicate receptive language are listening and reading (text, pictures, or signs). Words that indicate expressive language are speaking, writing, and demonstrating.

Language Function and Language Demands

Language demands are the certain ways that academic language is used as the students engage in the learning tasks. The language demands include:

- language function – purpose or reason for using language in tasks and is represented by action verb within the learning outcome
- vocabulary – words and phrases used within disciplines
- syntax – set of conventions for putting together symbols, words, and phrases into structures; example, syntax is the structure of sentences
- discourse – this is how individuals of a particular discipline talk and write; this is the structure of oral and written language

Below is a table with few academic language functions, students' use, and tasks associated with academic language function.

Academic Language Function	Students' Use	Tasks Associated With Academic Language Function
Seeking Information	observe and explore; acquire information	define, count, draw, indicate, list, name, point, recall, recite, repeat, write, state, select
Inform	identify or describe information	retell, recount, give, draw, conclude, explain, rewrite, summarize
Compare	describe similarities and differences	compare, contrast, identify, separate, point out, recognize, separate, attributes, differentiate,
Order	sequence objects, ideas, or events	organize, complete, process, outline, order
Classify	group objects or ideas according to their characteristics	break down, arrange, categorize, include create, generate, summarize, criteria, arrange, group
Analyze	separate whole into parts; identify relationships and patterns	analyze, contrast, calculate, criteria, categorize, discriminate, classify, deduce, detect, discriminate, distinguish, group, identify, infer, order, select, transform
Infer	make inferences; predict implications, hypothesize	predict, supporting, representing, restate, summarize, reconstruct, explain, create, synthesize, derive
Solve Problems	define and represent a problem; determine solution	solve, deduce, decide, table, refer, relationship, measure, relate, validate, support, test
Evaluate	assess and verify the worth of an object, idea, or decision	argue, compare, critique, grade, judge, justify, write, recommend, test, support, interpret, decide, describe, determine, distinguish

edTPA® Requirement of Academic Language

In the lesson plans, the candidates must include activities that involve a language function and language demands. The commentary for planning will require the candidates to document a language function and learning task(s) that give the students opportunities to practice using language function. When instructing, the candidates want to video record activities associated with using a language function in the learning process. In assessing tasks, the candidates will be required to provide evidence of students' understanding and use of an academic language function and demands. The assessment commentary questions may ask for examples of students understanding and using academic language.

This page is intentionally left blank.

Chapter 11 - Explanation of Planning Commentary

Candidates are required to complete the planning commentary related to the lesson plans, instructional materials, and assessments developed in Task 1. The commentary includes pre-typed questions that need responses. In this chapter, the candidates acquire information on how to write responses and gain further explanations to the commentary questions.

Due to copyright laws, this handbook will not copy paste the questions from the edTPA® handbooks. Instead, a description of the question is written. The candidates are recommended to have a copy of the assessment handbook when reviewing this chapter.

This chapter covers the following:

- Central Focus
- Knowledge of Students to Inform Teaching
- Supporting Students' Learning
- Supporting Development Through Language
- Monitoring Student Learning

Central Focus

Part A: Describe the central focus and the purpose for teaching.

Explanation: The candidates need to clearly state the central focus (Example: "The central focus is for the students to…"). The candidates need to state the purpose for teaching the topic. If multiple reasons exist for teaching the content, the candidates may consider using bullet points. Some candidates provide a summary of each lesson, which is not the correct way to answer the question.

Part B: Describe how the standards and learning objectives address the requirement of the central focus for the particular edTPA® subject assessments. Each edTPA® subject area has different requirements for the central focus.

Explanation: Some students discuss how their objectives address the requirements for the central focus, but fail to document how standards address the requirements of the central focus. One approach is to organize response by lesson plans.

Part C: Explain the connection between the lesson plans.

Explanation: The best way to answer this question is by breaking the answer into sections; one section per lesson plan. Explain in each section the intent of the lesson and how that lesson is connected with the other lessons. In each section, the candidates can explain how information learned from the previous lesson is needed to be successful.

Knowledge of Students to Inform Teaching

Part A: Document prior knowledge in relation to current students' knowledge, activities they can perform, and knowledge still acquiring.

Explanation: The purpose of this question is only to provide background knowledge of the students related to the central focus. Many candidates fail to answer the three parts to the question: knowledge students' possess, activities they can perform, and knowledge still in the learning process. In this response, the candidates can document what some students know and what others do not. Moreover, the candidates can discuss separately the knowledge of special education students, activities they can perform, and knowledge still developing.

Part B: Relate the central focus to personal/cultural/community assets.

Explanation: In this question, the candidates need to address the following:

- document the cultural backgrounds of the students, community, and economic status (low class, middle class, etc.)
- everyday experiences; this can be a long response, but the candidates want to relate everyday experience to the central focus and/or lesson activities
- interests; document the various interests that the students have, but make sure that there is a connection to the central focus and/or lesson activities

Supporting Students' Learning

Part A: Document connections of learning tasks with prior knowledge, personal/cultural/community assets, and theory.

Explanation: Responses need to clearly state how students' prior knowledge is connected to the lessons for the learning segment. Information needs to be written that these lessons are appropriate for the students, documenting the necessary background knowledge of the students. Explain how the activities in the lessons are related to past experiences or interests of the students. Most importantly, the candidates need to write in detail how learning tasks are related to research and theories. This latter requirement is missed by many students as they fail to write in good detail the connection of the tasks to learning theories. Not referencing theories/research will cause points to be reduced.

Part B: Explain how instructional strategies and planned supports are acceptable for the students.

Explanation: The key here is to address both strategies and supports. Examples of supports are visuals aides, computer programs, timers, calculator, peer tutors, large clocks, and graphic organizers. Examples of instructional strategies are direct modeling, think-pair-share activities, repetition, scaffolding instruction, cooperative learning, creative thinking, reflective activities, or simulations. The purpose of this question is to explain how both instructional strategies and planned supports are appropriate for:

- the whole class
- individuals
- English learners
- students with specific learning needs

The best way to respond is in four bullet points, with one for each of the above groups. In each bullet point, indicate how the supports and the instructional strategies are appropriate.

Part C: Describe common developmental approximations and common misconceptions regarding the central focus learning activities and how to address them.

Explanation: Using a bullet point format, document at least three common developmental approximations and/or common misconceptions. A common mistake by the candidates is failing to provide good responses on how to address the developmental approximations and/or common misconceptions.

Supporting Development Through Language

Part A: Identify one language function associated with achieving the central focus.

Explanation: Candidates make the mistake of mentioning more than one language function. In addition, candidates provide more information than required. A simple sentence is enough (ex. The language function of _____ will be used to support the student in achieving the central focus.).

Part B: Identify a key learning task that allows the students to use the language function.

Explanation: Candidates need to select a task that is meaningful and strongly supports the student in achieving the objectives of the lesson, ultimately supporting the achievement of the central focus. Simple sentences should be enough (ex. The key learning task that allows the students to use the language function is … This is planned in lesson __.).

Part C: Document the language demands the students need to understand and use for the language function and learning task identified.

Explanation: See Chapter 10 to respond to this question. The key is to directly answer the question and not provide unnecessary details.

Part D: Describe instructional supports that assist the students in using language function and language demands.

Explanation: The best way to respond to this question is to use a bullet point format to document the instructional support, and next to each support explain how the support can contribute in students successfully using language function and language demands.

Monitoring Student Learning

Part A: Describe formal and informal assessments that provide evidence of learning.

Explanation: Use the structure below to respond. Make sure to include details about each of the assessments listed.

Lesson 1

Formal Assessments include...

Informal Assessments include...

Lesson 2

Formal Assessments include...

Informal Assessments include...

Lesson 3

Formal Assessments include...

Informal Assessments include...

Part B: Explain how the assessments support the students with learning needs.

Explanation: Provide detail response on how the assessments support the students with specific needs, IEPs, 504 plans, English language learners, struggling readers, or gifted students. If any focus learner has a learning disability, this is good opportunity to explain how assessments support the focus student(s).

Chapter 12 - Explanation of Instruction Commentary

Candidates are required to complete the instruction commentary for the video recording submitted for the edTPA® portfolio. The commentary includes pre-typed questions that need responses. In this chapter, the candidates acquire information on how to write responses and gain further explanations on commentary questions.

Due to copyright laws, this handbook will not copy paste the questions from the edTPA® handbooks. Instead, a description of the question is written. The candidates are recommended to have a copy of the assessment handbook when reviewing this chapter.

This chapter will cover the following:

- Prompting a Positive Learning Environment
- Engaging Students in Learning
- Deepening Student Learning During Instruction
- Analyzing Teaching

A requirement of the instruction commentary is to time reference the video clip(s) given for grading. Suggestion for time referencing is indicate in parenthesis (clip 1: timestamp: 3:34). Candidates need to time reference as much as possible when writing the instruction commentary.

Prompting a Positive Learning Environment

Part A: Explain how instruction shows respect, rapport, and responsiveness to the students along with challenging the students to engage.

Explanation: The response needs to explain details regarding all instances of the candidates showing respect, rapport, and responsiveness to the students. These instances needs to be included in the video submitted and all instances must be time referenced. The candidates need to explain how the instances show respect, rapport, or responsiveness. Including instances of respect, rapport, and responsiveness that are not included in the video are acceptable to a limitation. Most of the response needs to be related to the video submitted. Make efforts to have at least 4 instances showing respect, rapport, and/or responsiveness along with challenging the students to engage.

Engaging Students in Learning

Part A: Explain how the candidates engaged students in learning to acquire skills.

Explanation: The response needs to indicate all instances in the video where the candidates engage the students in learning and acquiring skills. Candidates need to explain how the engagement occurred in detail and explain how the students acquired skills. The more instances described from the video the better chance to increase scores.

Part B: Link students' prior learning and personal, cultural, and community assets to instruction.

Explanation: This question is related to the question in the planning commentary Part A of Supporting Students in Learning. The intent of this question, in the instruction commentary, is to explain what was mentioned in the planning commentary was actually used during instructing students.

Deepening Student Learning During Instruction

Part A: Explain the methods used to elicit and build on students' responses to encourage thinking and applying skills.

Explanation: The best way to respond to this question is in bullet point format explaining all instances in the video that show the candidates seeking responses from the students and encouraging deeper thinking.

Part B: The question for this part will vary from edTPA® subjects. In general, the question requires the candidates to describe instances of supporting the students to achieve the central focus.

Explanation: The best way to respond to this question is in bullet point format explaining all instances in the video that show the candidates supporting the students to achieve the central focus.

Analyzing Teaching

Part A: Recommend changes to instruction to better support the students to achieve the central focus.

Explanation: The best way to respond to this question is in bullet point format explaining the recommended changes. Best approach is to select a change that impacts the entire class, a change for the student(s) with learning disability, and a change for English learners. In this question, the candidates should not explain how the change better supports the students as the question only asks for a list of changes.

Part B: The candidates need to explain why the recommended changes promote improvement.

Explanation: The best way to respond to this question is in bullet point format explaining how the recommended changes promote better learning. Each recommended change must be supported by evidence of students' learning, theory, and/or research.

Chapter 13 - Explanation of Assessment Commentary

Candidates are required to complete the assessment commentary to show students' progression toward the central focus. The commentary includes pre-typed questions that need responses. In this chapter, the candidates acquire information on how to write responses and gain further explanations on commentary questions.

Due to copyright laws, this book will not copy paste the questions from the edTPA® handbooks. Instead, a description of the question is written. The candidates are recommended to have a copy of the assessment handbook when reviewing this chapter.

This chapter will cover the following:

- Analyzing Student Learning
- Feedback to Guide Further Learning
- Evidence of Language Understanding and Use
- Using Assessment to Inform Instruction

Analyzing Student Learning

Part A: Identify learning objectives associated with the common assessment.

Explanation: The candidates only need to document the objectives that are reflected in the common assessment. Candidates make the mistake of including all the objectives.

Part B: Provide a graphic or a narrative summarizing students' performances on the common assessment.

Explanation: If the candidates used a rubric system for the evaluation criteria, the best approach is to develop a table or chart depicting the overall performance on the common assessment. If the candidates select to write a narrative, the response needs to address all the evaluation criteria in the rubric and discuss the entire class performance.

Part C: Use student work samples and entire class summary to analyze learning patterns.

Explanation: In the response, the following are considerations to take into account:

- patterns of learning for the entire class
- patterns of learning for the focus students
- patterns of learning for students with disability
- compare entire class performance vs. focus students
- compare focus students vs. students with disability
- compare entire class vs. students with disability
- if there is/are a English language learner student(s), the candidates can make comparison with different groups

Feedback to Guide Further Learner

Part A: Identify the format of feedback provided to the focus students.

Explanation: Simply select one of the options provided in the commentary question.

Part B: Explain how feedback is connected to learners' strengths and needs relative to the learning objectives measured.

Explanation: Many students discuss feedback related to all the learning objectives. The intent of the question is to only discuss objectives assessed in the evaluation criteria. The best way to respond to the question is to break it down by students (not all students, only the students for which feedback is submitted in the edTPA® portfolio), and for each student discuss how the feedback is connected to individual strengths and needs.

Part C: Discuss how candidates will support each focus student to comprehend and use the feedback.

Explanation: The best way to answer this is by breaking it down for each student and discussing the following for each student (only the students for which feedback is submitted in the edTPA® portfolio):

- explain how to support the student in understanding the feedback
- use of feedback within learning segment
- use of feedback to develop the student in future lessons

Evidence of Language Understanding and Use

Part A: Explain and provide examples of how the students used or struggled using academic language function and academic language demands.

Explanation: Many candidates respond to this question for only the focus students; however, the candidates can also reference any student from the learning segment. This question also gives the candidates opportunity to provide additional video on language use, and the recommendation is to make all efforts to provide a video of the students involved in using the academic language function. The best way to respond to this question is to discuss each of the focus students and make sure to reference work samples, Task 2 video(s), and additional language use video. Also, discuss several additional students in the classroom and reference Task 2 video and the additional language use video. Detail examples are desired for this question.

Using Assessment to Inform Instruction

Part A: Discuss next lessons for instruction to promote further learning.

Explanation: The best way to respond to this question is by using bullet point form.

- For the entire class, the next steps for instruction include…
- For focus student 1, the next steps for instruction include…
- For focus student 2, the next steps for instruction include…
- For focus student 3, the next steps for instruction include…
- For students with learning disability, the next steps for instruction include…

Part B: Give reason for the next steps identified. The candidates need to reference research and/or theory.

Explanation: The best way to respond is having one bullet point for each of the next steps of instruction discussed above. Explain in detail how students' performance and the theory/research are related to next steps of instruction.

This page is intentionally left blank.

Chapter 14 - Special Education edTPA®

The Special Education edTPA® requires the candidates to select one student (known as the focus learner) with multiple learning needs to analyze during the planning, instructing, and assessing. The candidates will identify one learning goal and develop 3-5 consecutive lesson plans and provide supports related to the goal. In selecting the learning goal, the candidates can select a goal related to:

- academic content area related to an Individualized Education Program (IEP) goal
- academic content area if no academic IEP goals exist
- a goal in the IEP

The goal of the edTPA® Special Education assessment is for the candidates to demonstrate their ability to teach students with multiple learning needs. This chapter includes a complete edTPA® assessment portfolio for the Special Education subject area.

This chapter covers the following:

- Assessments/Baseline Data
- edTPA® Example and Reference Note
- Task 1: Part A – Context for Learning Information
- Task 1: Part B – Lesson Plans for Learning Segment
- Task 1: Part C – Instructional Material
- Task 1: Part D – Assessments and/or Data Collection Procedures
- Task 1: Part E – Planning Commentary
- Task 2: Part A – Video Clips
- Task 2: Part B – Instruction Commentary
- Task 3: Part A – Work Samples
- Task 3: Part B – Completed Daily Assessment Records and Baseline Data
- Task 3: Part C – Evidence of Feedback
- Task 3: Part D – Assessment Commentary
- Special Education Scores and Evaluation Analysis

Assessments/Baseline Data

Baseline data is showing the focus learner's level of pre-instructional knowledge. The candidates need to have an understanding of what information the student already knows related to the learning goal and associated objectives. For example, if the student is learning how to add numbers within 20s, an example of baseline data can be a pre-assessment test on adding numbers within 10s and few questions of adding numbers within 20s. If the student is learning how to read second grade level stories, a running record on the student reading first grade level stories is appropriate as baseline data. Another example, if the student is learning to write paragraphs, appropriate baseline data might be an activity that requires the student to construct sentences and short paragraphs. Baseline data needs to be related to the learning goal/associated objectives. The baseline data is used for comparison purposes with assessments giving during the learning segment. Baseline data can be in many forms, such as:

- teacher made test
- observational notes
- curriculum-based measures
- task analysis assessment
- prior instructional history
- IEP performance against goals

Apart of the Special Education edTPA®, the candidates are also required to submit all daily assessment records for the focus learner with the baseline data in Task 3 Part B. Daily assessment records are tools that allow the candidates to monitor focus student's progress toward the learning goal.

edTPA® Example and Reference Note

In this chapter, a Special Education edTPA® is included with a first grade student as the focus learner. The portfolio is an unedited example, so the portfolio does include grammar, punctuation, and usage errors. All documents that are submitted for the real edTPA® submission are included except for the video. Instead, a summary of the video is provided.

NOTE: Due to copyright laws, the this book does not use direct wording/questions from the edTPA® handbook. Templates (and wording) provided by SCALE are not used and direct content/questions from templates and commentaries are not used. Candidates are recommended to have copy of the assessment handbook when reviewing this chapter.

Task 1: Part A – Context for Learning Information

Context for Learning

Part A

I teach a first grade math and literacy classroom with 12 students at an under-performed elementary school. For four of those students, I provide additional instruction after school. For the edTPA®, instruction will take place after school in an open room at the school library. My role in the focus learner's instructional program is to instruct math and literacy curriculums. I teach both math and literacy along with providing support for behavioral management. This learning segment will occur afterschool for 1 hour on Tuesdays and Thursdays. The primary language of instruction of the focus learner is English.

Part B

There are no additional third party requirements or expectations that impact planning, instructing, and assessing.

Part C

For math, the textbook is "Go Math! Multi-Volume Student Edition Grade 1." The publisher is Houghton Mifflin Harcourt, and the date of publication is 2015. For this learning segment, this textbook is not used.

Part D

There are four students in the group I am instructing. One student is an English language learner, two learners are with IEP, and one student is a general education learner.

About the Focus Learner

- Age: 6
- Gender: Male
- Grade level: First grade
- Primary Language: English
- The focus learner has dyslexia, dyscalculia, and ADHD.
- No augmentative or alternative communication used for the learner.
- The focus learner's behavior management plans recommend that he not remain sitting in one setting for more than 1 hour. Recommendation is to have him walk around the classroom or have him engage in activity requiring movement.

Task 1: Part B – Lesson Plans for Learning Segment

Lesson One

Lesson Title – Adding Within Twenties

Grade Level – First Grade

Learning Goal

Gain knowledge in adding and subtracting within 20 to be able to solve word problems requiring addition and subtraction within 20.

Educational Standards

Educational standards related to the instruction of this lesson include:

-   1.OA.6 Add and subtract within 20, demonstrating fluency for addition and subtraction within 10.

Lesson Objectives

The objective of the lesson is to gain knowledge of adding within 20.

Instructional Material/Resources

The instructional material/resources include a whiteboard, blocks, and worksheets.

Identification of Students Prerequisite Knowledge and Skills

In order for the students to be successful in the learning segment, having knowledge of the following is necessary: understand the concept of addition, recognize the symbol of addition, mastery in adding within 10

Instructional Procedures (step by step instructional procedures)

Step 1: I will start by welcoming the students to the afterschool instruction. Also, I will inform the students of the objectives and expectations, so they have understanding of the lesson purpose. In particular, I will communicate to the students that there will be a worksheet assignment at the end of the lesson, and 80% or higher is considered passing.

Step 2: To activate students' prior knowledge, I will call on students to respond to the following questions:

-   Explain the concept of addition.
-   What is the sign used for addition?
-   2+4 =, 4+3 = and 1+3 =

These questions will be written on the whiteboard, and as the students respond, I will write the responses on the whiteboard.

Step 3: I will explain to the students that I will be using various methods to add within 20. These methods include: object method (this is using blocks to add), tally mark method (this is using tally marks), and finger method (this is using fingers to add)

Step 4: I will start by showing the students the object method with two numbers. On the whiteboard, I will write "9 + 3 =". I will place 9 black square blocks and 3 blue square blocks on the round table. After that, I will ask the students to count the total number of blocks with me. To engage the students, I will write a problem on the whiteboard, "4 + 6 =", and have a student come up with the answers using the blocks.

Step 5: The next method that I will show is the tally mark method with two numbers. On the whiteboard, I will write "8 + 4 =". Using the whiteboard, I will write down 8 tally marks with a black marker and 4 tally marks with a blue marker. With the students, I will count aloud the total number of tally marks. To engage the students, I will do a pair activity related to the tally method. I will have the students complete a worksheet with two questions (2 + 11 = ? and 7 + 7 = ?), and I will give them 5 minutes to come up with the answers. Once completed, the students will share the answers.

Step 6: The last method I will show is the finger method with two numbers. On the whiteboard, I will put "8 + 5 =". With my hands, I will show 8 fingers and then add 5 fingers, counting out load. To check students' understanding, I will have the students complete an example problem (3 + 9 = ?). After that, I will write another problem (11 + 4 =) on the whiteboard for the students to attempt. I will ask the students to attempt the problem using the finger method. Students will realize that this method is not always the best approach as humans only have 10 fingers. I will communicate to the students that the finger method is not always the best approach to use.

Step 7: I will proceed in showing the students how to add with more than two numbers with the tally method and the object method. On the whiteboard, I will put "9 + 3 + 4 =". I will place 9 black square blocks, 3 blue square blocks, and 4 red blocks on the round table. After that, I will ask the students to count the total number of blocks with me. To engage the students, I will write a problem on the whiteboard, "4 + 6 + 3 =" and have one student come up with the answers using blocks.

Step 8: Next, I will use the tally method to show the students how to add with more than two numbers. On the whiteboard, I will put "8 + 4 + 3 =". Using the whiteboard, I will write down 8 tally marks with a black marker, 4 tally marks with a blue marker, and 3 tally marks with a red marker. With the students, I will count aloud the total number of tally marks. To engage the students, I will write an example problem (6 + 6 + 6 = ?) on the whiteboard and call on a student to work out problem on the whiteboard.

Closure Procedures

To recap learning, I will write the following problems on the whiteboard: 11 + 6 =, 15 + 4 =, 9 + 7 + 2 + 1 =, and 14 + 5. I will call on the students to show how to solve the problem using the method they think is the best.

I will have the students complete a worksheet. Once completed, I will give the students a red marker for self-grading purposes. I will go over each question and have the students correct themselves on their paper. I will collect all papers to document the grades.

Guided Practice/Independent Practice/Planned Supports/Communication Skill

Guided Practice – As I instruct, I plan to show example problems. I also plan to have the students provide guidance to each other when working on paired activity. When the students show signs of struggling, I will guide the students in reaching the correct answers.

Independent Practice – I plan to have the students work independently on example problems. I also plan to call the students to the whiteboard to show how to complete the problem(s) independently.

Planned Support – The planned supports include:

Whiteboard – I plan to write all problems on the whiteboard for my focus learner to support him in learning due to his dyslexia and dyscalculia disabilities. Visualization is a way to support him in processing information.

Paired Activity – The paired activities allows movement and engagement, which supports my focus learner from a behavioral standpoint.

Scaffolding – I will start the students off by reviewing the concept of addition, then adding with two numbers, and then proceeding to adding with more than two numbers.

Communication Skill – The communication skill that will be required is answering questions through the principal of counting.

Differentiated Instruction

Two of my students are visual students, so I will use different color blocks. Engaging students, having paired activities, and calling on students supported my focus learner in moving around and communicating with other students.

Generalization, maintenance, and self-directed

Generalization – I plan to have the students use what they learned from adding two numbers to the situation of adding more than two numbers.

Maintenance – I will have the students complete activities right after I teach them and at the conclusion of the lesson, which supports them in maintaining knowledge.

Self-directed – I will have students grade their own worksheet. I will have the students struggle to complete "11 + 4 =" with the finger method, allowing them to see that it is not always the best approach to use.

Assessments

Informal Assessment – I will be observing students' behavior in using blocks, fingers, and tallies to see if they understand the information being presented to them.

Formal Assessment – Students will complete a worksheet, which will confirm learning of the objective.

Lesson 2

Lesson Title – Subtracting Within Twenties

Grade Level – First Grade

Learning Goal

Gain knowledge in adding and subtracting within 20 to be able to solve word problems requiring addition and subtraction within 20.

Educational Standards

Educational standards related to the instruction of this lesson include:

- 1.OA.6 Add and subtract within 20, demonstrating fluency for addition and subtraction within 10.

Lesson Objectives

The objective of the lesson is to gain knowledge of subtracting within 20.

Instructional Material/Resources

The instructional material/resources include a whiteboard, blocks, and worksheets.

Identification of Students Prerequisite Knowledge and Skills

In order for the students to be successful in the learning segment, having knowledge of the following is necessary: understand the concept of subtracting, recognize the symbol of subtracting, and mastery in subtracting within 10.

Instructional Procedures (step by step instructional procedures)

Step 1: I will start by welcoming the students to the afterschool instruction. Also, I will inform the students of the objectives and expectations, so they have understanding of the purpose of the lesson. In particular, I will communicate to the students that there will be a worksheet assignment at the end of the lesson, and 80% or higher is considered passing.

Step 2: To activate students' prior knowledge, I will call on the students to respond to the following questions:

- Explain the concept of subtraction.
- What is the sign used for subtraction?
- $5 - 3 =$, $8 - 4 =$, and $7 - 4 =$

These questions will be written on the whiteboard, and as the students respond, I will write the responses on the whiteboard.

Step 3: I will explain to the students, I will be using two methods. These methods include: object method (this is using blocks to subtract) and tally mark method (this is using tally marks on sheet of paper).

Step 4: I will start by showing the students the object method with two numbers. On the whiteboard, I will write "17 - 3 =". I will place 17 black square blocks on the round table. After that, I will remove three blocks from the table. To engage students, I will write a problem on the whiteboard, "19 - 3 =" and have a student come up with the answer using the blocks.

Step 5: The next method that will be shown to the students is the tally mark method with two numbers. On the whiteboard, I will put "18 - 4 =". Using the whiteboard, I will write down 18 tally marks with a black marker. Using a blue marker, I will cross out 4 tally marks. With the students, I will count aloud the total number of tally marks. To engage students, I will do a pair activity related to the tally method. I will have the students complete a worksheet with two questions (12 - 1 = ? and 18 - 7 = ?), and I will give them 5 minutes to come up with the answers. Once completed, the students will share the responses.

Step 6: I will write the following on the whiteboard: 18 – 5 = ? and 16 – 4 = ?. I will ask the students if using the finger method is the best approach to solving these questions.

Step 7: I will proceed in showing the students how to subtract with more than two numbers using the tally method and object method. On the whiteboard, I will write "19 - 3 - 4 =". I will have one student place 19 square blocks on the round table, one student remove 3 square blocks, one student remove 4 blocks, and one student count the remaining blocks.

Step 8: Next, I will use the tally method to show the students how to subtract with more than two numbers. On the whiteboard, I will write "18 - 2 - 3 =". Using the whiteboard, I will write down 18 tally marks with a black marker. Using a red marker, I will ask the students what to do next and guide them in achieving the answer. With the students, I will count aloud the total number of remaining tally marks.

Closure Procedures

To recap learning, I will write the following problems on the whiteboard: 19 - 6 =, 15 - 4 =, 15 - 3 - 2 =, and 16 – 5 =. I will call on the students to show how to solve the problem using the method they think is best.

I will have the students complete a worksheet. Once completed, I will give the students a red marker for self-grading purposes. I will go over each question and have the students correct themselves on their paper. I will collect all papers to document the grades.

Guided Practice/Independent Practice/Planned Supports/Communication Skill

Guided Practice – As I instruct, I plan to show example problems. I also plan to have the students reach the final answers with my guidance during instruction. When the students show signs of struggling, I will guide the students in reaching the correct answers.

Independent Practice – I plan to have the students work independently on example problems. I also plan to call the students up to the whiteboard to show how to complete the problem independently.

Planned Support – The planned supports include:

Whiteboard – I plan to write all problems on the whiteboard for my focus learner to support him in learning due to his dyslexia and dyscalculia disabilities. Visualization is a way to support him in processing information.

Scaffolding – I will start the students off by reviewing the concept of subtraction, then subtracting with two numbers, and then proceeding to subtracting more than two numbers.

Communication Skill – The communication skill that will be required is answering questions through the principal of counting.

Differentiated Instruction

Two of my students are visual students, so I used different color markers. Engaging students, having paired activities, and calling on students supported my focus learner in moving around and communicating with other students.

Generalization, maintenance, and self-directed

Generalization – I plan to have the students use what they learned from subtracting two numbers to the situation of subtracting more than two numbers.

Maintenance – I will have the students complete activities right after I teach them and at the conclusion of the lesson, which supports them in maintaining knowledge.

Self-directed – I will have the students grade their own worksheet. I also call on the students to support me in reaching the final answer to example problems during instruction.

Assessments

Informal Assessment – I will be observing students' behavior in using blocks and tallies to see if they understand the information being presented to them.

Formal Assessment – At the end of the lesson, the students will complete a worksheet, which will confirm learning of the objective.

Lesson 3

Lesson Title – Mix Review Subtraction and Addition

Grade Level – First Grade

Learning Goal

The following is the learning goal related to student's IEP:

Gain knowledge in adding and subtracting within 20 to be able to solve word problems requiring addition and subtraction within 20.

Educational Standards

Educational standards related to the instruction of this lesson include:

- 1.OA.6 Add and subtract within 20, demonstrating fluency for addition and subtraction within 10.

Lesson Objectives

The objective of the lesson is to gain knowledge of adding and subtracting together within 20.

Instructional Material/Resources

The instructional material/resources include a whiteboard, blocks, and worksheets.

Identification of Students Prerequisite Knowledge and Skills

In order for the students to be successful in the learning segment, the students need to have knowledge of adding within 20 and subtracting within 20, which are acquired in lesson one and two.

Instructional Procedures (step by step instructional procedures)

Step 1: I will start by welcoming the students to the afterschool instruction. Also, I will inform the students of the objectives and expectations, so they have understanding of the lesson's purpose. In particular, I will communicate to the students that there will be a worksheet assignment at the end of the lesson, and that 80% or higher is considered passing. I will also recap the learning from the two previous lessons and explain the connection of the current lesson to the previous lessons. Since this lesson is a combination of the previous two lessons, I will also explain to the students that they will be the teachers of the day by explaining how to complete various math problems.

Step 2: To activate the students' prior knowledge, I will call on the students to respond to the following math problems:

- $18 - 3 =$
- $14 + 2 =$
- $20 - 2 =$

- 16 + 2 =

These questions will be written on the whiteboard, and as the students respond, I will write the responses on the whiteboard.

Step 3: On the whiteboard, I will write "19 – 3 + 2 =". I will ask one student to show how to complete the problem using the block method. I will ask the student to verbally explain each step being performing. If the student is struggling, I will ask one of the classmates to support the student by asking about the next step to complete the problem. Once the student has reached the final answers, I will ask another student to tell me if the answer is correct.

Step 4: On the whiteboard, I will write "17 + 2 – 7 =". I will ask one student to show how to complete the problem using the tally method. I will ask the student to explain each step as he/she is performing the step. If the student is struggling, I will ask one of the classmates to support the student. Once the student has reached the final answers, I will ask another student to tell me if the answer is correct.

Step 5: On the whiteboard, I will write "10 + 2 + 3 – 6 =". I will ask one student to show how to complete the problem using the tally method. I will ask the student to explain each step as they are performing the step. If the student is struggling, I will ask one of the classmates to support the student. Once the student has reached the final answers, I will ask another student to tell me if the answer is correct.

Step 6: On the whiteboard, I will write "11 + 1 + 3 – 5 =". I will ask one student to show how to complete the problem using the block method. I will ask the student to explain each step as they are performing the step. If the student is struggling, I will ask one of the classmates to support the student. Once the student has reached the final answers, I will ask another student to tell me if the answer is correct.

Closure Procedures

To recap learning, I will put the following problems on the whiteboard: 19 – 6 + 3 =, 17 - 4 + 3 =, 15 - 3 + 2 =, and 16 – 5 + 5 =. I will call on the students to show how to solve the problem using the method they think is best.

I will have the students complete a worksheet. Once completed, I will give the students a red marker for self-grading purposes. I will go over each question and have the students correct themselves on their paper. I will collect all papers to document the grades.

Guided Practice/Independent Practice/Planned Supports/Communication Skill

Guided Practice – I will let the students be the teacher. As the students struggle in obtaining the right answers, I will have peers intervene to provide support.

Independent Practice – The activity involves the students to be the teacher, giving them ample independent opportunities to teach and learn.

Planned Support – The planned supports include:

Whiteboard – I plan to write all problems on the whiteboard to support my focus learner as he has dyslexia and dyscalculia as seeing the problem supports him in learning.

Peers – When the students struggle in achieving the answers, peers will engage to support the students.

Communication Skill – The communication skill that will be required is answering questions through the principal of counting.

Differentiated Instruction

Engaging the students and calling on the students supported my focus learner in moving around and communicating with other students.

Generalization, maintenance, and self-directed

Generalization – Students will learn how to add within 20 in one lesson and then will learn how to subtract within 20 another lesson. In this lesson, they will use that knowledge in different instances of adding and subtracting within 20s together.

Maintenance – I plan to have the students be the teachers in this lesson. As they struggle, they will be guided by peers. Struggle is a way to maintaining knowledge.

Self-directed – I will have the students grade their own worksheet. Students will be independently teaching their peers.

Assessments

Informal Assessment – I will be observing the students as they explain how to do the problem to their peers.

Formal Assessment – At the end of the lesson, the students will complete a worksheet, which will confirm learning of the objective.

Lesson 4

Lesson Title – Solving Word Problems

Grade Level – First Grade

Learning Goal

Gain knowledge in adding and subtracting within 20 to be able to solve word problems requiring addition and subtraction within 20.

Educational Standards

Educational standards related to the instruction of this lesson include:

- 1.OA.1 Use addition and subtraction within 20 to solve word problems involving situations of adding to, taking from, putting together, taking apart, and comparing, with unknowns in all positions, e.g., by using objects, drawings, and equations with a symbol for the unknown number to represent the problem.
- 1.OA.6 Add and subtract within 20, demonstrating fluency for addition and subtraction within 10.
- 1.OA.2 Solve word problems that call for addition of three whole numbers whose sum is less than or equal to 20, e.g., by using objects, drawings, and equations with a symbol for the unknown number to represent the problem.

Lesson Objectives

The objective of the lesson is to solve basic word problems involving addition, subtraction, or addition and subtracting together within 20.

Instructional Material/Resources

The instructional material/resources include a whiteboard, blocks, and worksheets.

Identification of Students Prerequisite Knowledge and Skills

In order for the student to be successful in the learning segment, the students need to have knowledge of adding within 20 and subtracting within 20.

Instructional Procedures (step by step instructional procedures)

Step 1: I will start by welcoming the students to the afterschool instruction. Also, I will inform the students of the objectives and expectations, so they have understanding of the lesson's purpose. In particular, I will communicate that there will be a worksheet assignment at the end of the lesson, and 80% or higher is considered passing

Step 2: To activate the students' prior knowledge, I will pair two students to complete math problems using block method and the other two students using tally method. Once the students complete, the students will compare answers. The problems they will complete are

- 18 – 3 + 4 =
- 14 + 2 – 1 =
- 20 – 7 + 3 =
- 16 + 2 - 3 =

Step 3: To start the lesson, I will teach the students keywords that are associated with addition and subtraction. I will have a poster ready to show and will display throughout the duration of the lesson.

Step 4: I will show the students how to solve a word problem and the key takeaway points. I will write on the whiteboard: "Juan has 2 red cakes, 4 blue cakes, and 9 white cakes. How many total cakes does Juan have?" I will emphasize the importance of reading carefully and looking for keywords in solving word problems. I will ask the students the following questions:

- What is the question asking to find?
- What operation(s) is/are involved?
- What is/are the keyword(s) in the question?

On the whiteboard, I will write down red cake, blue cake, and white cake. I will call on the students to tell me how many tally marks I need to put under each one. Once completed, one student will be called to give the final answer.

Step 5: I will write on the whiteboard: "Kate has 19 pencils. She gave 2 to Max and 4 to Berry. How many pencils does Kate have left?" I will emphasize the importance of reading carefully and looking for keywords in solving word problems. I will ask the students the following questions:

- What is the question asking to find?
- What operation(s) is/are involved?
- What is/are the keyword(s) in the question?

On the whiteboard, I will put 19 tally marks. I will ask the students how many to cross out for Max and Berry, and I will ask one student to give me the final answer.

Step 6: I will write on the whiteboard: "Lynn got 15 toys for Christmas, and he got 4 toys for his birthday. Lynn gave 2 toys to his sister. In school, he won 3 toys. How many total toys does Lynn have? I will emphasize the importance of reading carefully and looking for keywords in solving word problems. I will ask the students the following questions:

- What is the question asking to find?
- What operation(s) are involved?
- What is/are the keyword(s) in the question?

This time I will ask the students to tell me what to do to solve the problem. I will write correct information and guide the students in providing me with the correct information to solve the word problem.

Closure Procedures

To recap learning, I will ask the students to explain to me the importance aspect of solving word problems.

I will have the students complete a worksheet. Once completed, I will collect the papers and grade the papers.

Guided Practice/Independent Practice/Planned Supports/Communication Skill

Guided Practice – I have the students tell me what to write on the board to achieve the correct answer. If the students provide inaccurate information, I guide them in providing the correct steps.

Independent Practice – Students are required to complete a worksheet at the end of the lesson.

Planned Support – The planned supports include:

Whiteboard – I plan to write all problems on the whiteboard for my focus learner to support him in learning due to his dyslexia and dyscalculia disabilities. Visualization is a way to support him in processing information.

Poster – I will have a poster with keywords associated with adding and subtracting. The poster will be displayed during the entire lesson.

Communication Skill – The communication skill that will be required is answering questions through the principal of counting.

Differentiated Instruction

Two of my students are visual students, so I used different color markers. Engaging the students and calling on the students supported my focus learner in moving around and communicating with other students.

Generalization, maintenance, and self-directed

Generalization – Students will learn how to add within 20 alone and then learned how to subtract within 20 alone. In this lesson, they use that knowledge to solve word problems.

Maintenance – I plan to have the students answer questions and guide me in achieving the right answers. As they struggle, they will be guided by myself or peers. Struggle is a way to maintaining knowledge.

Self-directed – In the beginning of the lesson, I will have students complete a pair activity. Two students will work out the problems using block method while the other two students work out the problems using tally method. The students will compare answers for grading purposes.

Assessments

Informal Assessment – I will be observing students' behavior in using blocks and tallies to see if they understand the information being presented to them.

Formal Assessment – At the end of the lesson, the students will complete a worksheet, which will confirm learning of the objective.

Student Name:

Instructional Worksheet – Addition

Using the tally method, answer the following questions.

QUESTION 1

2 + 11 =

QUESTION 2

7 + 7 =

Student Name:

Instructional Worksheet – Subtraction

Using the tally method, answer the following questions.

QUESTION 1

12 – 1 =

QUESTION 2

18 – 7 =

Adding Keywords	Subtracting Keywords
1. Add	1. Take away
2. Altogether	2. Left
3. Both	3. Minus
4. In all	4. Give
5. Sum	5. Subtract
6. Total	6. Less

Lesson 1 – Assessment

Student Name:

Adding Within 20 – Worksheet

Directions: On separate sheet of paper, answer the follow questions.

QUESTION 1

Using the blocks, solve the following:

8 + 9 =

QUESTION 2

Using the blocks, solve the following:

17 + 2 =

QUESTION 3

Using the blocks, solve the following:

11 + 2 + 4 =

QUESTION 4

Using your fingers, solve the following:

9 + 3 =

QUESTION 5

Using your fingers, solve the following:

9 + 3 + 2 =

QUESTION 6

Using your fingers, solve the following:

12 + 3 =

QUESTION 7

Using the tally method, solve the following:

11 + 3 + 3 =

QUESTION 8

Using the tally method, solve the following:

14 + 2 + 3 =

QUESTION 9

Using the tally method, solve the following:

11 + 6 + 3 =

QUESTION 10

Using the tally method, solve the following:

3 + 14 =

Student Name:

Subtracting Within 20 – Worksheet

Directions: On separate sheet of paper, answer the follow questions.

QUESTION 1

Using the blocks, solve the following:

18 - 7 =

QUESTION 2

Using the blocks, solve the following:

17 - 2 =

QUESTION 3

Using the blocks, solve the following:

11 - 2 - 4 =

QUESTION 4

Using the blocks, solve the following:

19 - 3 =

QUESTION 5

Using the blocks, solve the following:

19 - 3 - 2 =

QUESTION 6

Using the tally method, solve the following:

19 - 12 - 2 =

QUESTION 7

Using the tally method, solve the following:

19 - 3 - 3 =

QUESTION 8

Using the tally method, solve the following:

14 - 2 - 1 =

QUESTION 9

Using the tally method, solve the following:

18 - 6 - 2 =

QUESTION 10

Using the tally method, solve the following:

19 - 7 =

Student Name:

Adding and Subtracting Within 20 – Worksheet

Directions: On separate sheet of paper, answer the follow questions.

QUESTION 1

Using the blocks, solve the following:

$18 - 9 + 5 =$

QUESTION 2

Using the blocks, solve the following:

$17 + 2 - 5 =$

QUESTION 3

Using the blocks, solve the following:

$11 + 2 - 4 =$

QUESTION 4

Using your fingers, solve the following:

$9 - 3 + 12 =$

QUESTION 5

Using the tally method, solve the following:

$19 - 3 + 2 =$

QUESTION 6

Using your fingers, solve the following:

$12 + 3 - 2 =$

QUESTION 7

Using the tally method, solve the following:

$11 - 3 + 3 =$

QUESTION 8

Using the tally method, solve the following:

$14 - 2 + 3 =$

QUESTION 9

Using the tally method, solve the following:

$11 + 6 - 3 =$

QUESTION 10

Using the tally method, solve the following:

$3 + 14 - 2 =$

Student Name:

Final Assessment

QUESTION 1

Solve the following problem using the block method (draw blocks):

11 + 9 =

QUESTION 2

Solve the following problem using the block method (draw blocks):

15 - 3 =

QUESTION 3

Solve the following problem using the block method (draw blocks):

14 - 4 + 3 =

QUESTION 4

Solve the following problem using your fingers:

5 + 7 - 5 =

QUESTION 5

Name three keywords associated with adding.

QUESTION 6

Martin has 14 coins. He gave three to Mary and two to Derrick. Derrick gave back one of his cards to Martin. How many total cards does Martin have left?

QUESTION 7

Name three keywords associated with subtracting.

QUESTION 8

Kathy has four apples, two strawberries, and four blueberries. How many fruits in total does Kathy have?

QUESTION 9

There are 14 books in the classroom. Four students take the book home and two do not return the books at the end of the school year. How many books are there in the classroom at the end of the school year?

QUESTION 10

Victor brought 17 flowers. He gave two to his mother and two to his sister. Victor also gave three flowers to his teacher. How many flowers does Victor have left?

Student Name:

Daily Assessment Record

LESSON NUMBER:

OBJECTIVE:

QUESTION 1

Did the student participate when called upon?

QUESTION 2

Did the student provide correct response majority of the time when asked questions?

QUESTION 3

How many times was the student incorrect?

QUESTION 4

Did the student engage with peers in learning?

QUESTION 5

What score did the student receive on the lesson worksheet?

Task 1: Part E – Planning Commentary

QUESTION 1

Part A

The answer to Part A is the following table:

Learning Goal: Gain knowledge in adding and subtracting within 20 to be able to solve word problems requiring addition and subtraction within 20.	
Relevant Academic Standards: - 1.OA.1 Use addition and subtraction within 20 to solve word problems involving situations of adding to, taking from, putting together, taking apart, and comparing, with unknowns in all positions, e.g., by using objects, drawings, and equations with a symbol for the unknown number to represent the problem. - 1.OA.6 Add and subtract within 20, demonstrating fluency for addition and subtraction within 10. - 1.OA.2 Solve word problems that call for addition of three whole numbers whose sum is less than or equal to 20, e.g., by using objects, drawings, and equations with a symbol for the unknown number to represent the problem.	
Lesson Objectives	**List of Planned Supports**
Lesson 1: The objective of the lesson is to gain knowledge of adding within 20. Lesson 2: The objective of the lesson is to gain knowledge of subtracting within 20. Lesson 3: The objective of the lesson is to gain knowledge of adding and subtracting within 20. Lesson 4: The objective of the lesson is to solve basic word problems involving addition, subtraction, or addition and subtracting together within 20.	Lesson 1: Whiteboard, Paired Activities, and Scaffolding Lesson 2: Whiteboard, Paired Activities, and Scaffolding Lesson 3: Whiteboard and Peers Lesson 4: Whiteboard and Poster

Part B

The learning goal is academic and aligned with the focus learner's IEP goal. The student has been diagnosed with dyscalculia (diagnosis is mild; improvements have been documented), and his IEP indicates to have activities that allow him to use and apply the concept of counting. In particular, the IEP encourages multiple approaches to solving problems to give the student opportunity to select preferred approach. The learning goal is aligned with the IEP as the student is involved in counting via addition and subtraction along with solving word problems. The student needs to be engaged in various activities. Instructional support materials assist in remaining on tasks and supporting his dyscalculia/ADHD. Having the student engage in peer activity and class discussion provides variety in instruction. Everything is written on the whiteboard, which will allow the student to refer back, in case he might forget. Blocks will be used as additional support to get the student engaged and encourage him to use different methods for solving problems.

Part C

No special accommodations or modifications were made to the learning environment, instruction, or assessments.

Part D

The focus learner has gained understanding of addition and subtraction when working within 10s. The student has worked on very basic word problems within 10s. This lesson connects with student's prior learning of counting and extends to apply to addition and subtraction within 20s.

The following will explain how the objectives, tasks, materials, and supports are sequenced to allow the focus learner to achieve IEP goals, standards, and the learning goal.

Lesson 1

Lesson 1 activities involve the operation of addition. Three methods will be introduced to increase student's ability to perform and remember adding within 20. Focus learner will complete in-class questions, paired activities, and worksheets to demonstrate learning. Modeling how to complete the operations and subsequently having the focus learner apply the learning will allow the student to retain the knowledge. In the early stages of math skills development, especially for the student with math learning disability, using objects engages and supports them in learning better and quicker. With my focus learner being visual, different color blocks are included for the purpose of getting the student involved in the learning process. The instruction is sequenced to start with adding just two numbers and then proceeds into adding more than two numbers. Doing so gives the student better chances of succeeding or quickly acquiring knowledge related to adding more than two numbers.

Lesson 2

Lesson 2 activities involve the operation of subtraction. Various methods will be introduced to increase student's ability to perform and remember subtracting within 20. Focus learner will complete in-class questions, paired activities, and worksheets to demonstrate learning. I will teach the student via modeling example problems. Following modeling, the student will be required to complete example problems, which will the student in showing learning toward objectives and standards along with retaining the information. In the early stages of math skill development, especially for the student with math learning disability, using objects engages and supports them in learning better and quicker. With my focus learner being visual, different color blocks were included for the purpose of getting the student involved in the learning process. Similar to Lesson 1, the instruction is sequenced to start with subtracting just two numbers and then proceeds into subtracting more than two numbers. Doing so gives the student better chances of succeeding or quickly acquiring knowledge related to subtracting more than two numbers.

Lesson 3

Lesson 3 involves the focus learner applying the knowledge of lesson one and lesson two together to solve math problems involving both adding and subtracting. Doing a combined lesson allows the student to show achievement on the academic standards related to both addition and subtraction. The learning tasks in this lesson involve the students' being the teacher. This will give my focus learner more responsibility of learning as explaining to others how to do activities increasing chances of remembering the information. When the student is teaching, if he has difficulty, his peers will be the support system to get him to the right direction.

Lesson 4

Lesson 4 involves the students completing word problems, which is related to academic standard: 1.OA.1 – Use addition and subtraction within 20 to solve word problems. By having the students do addition operations then subtraction operations and then both addition and subtraction mixed together, the sequence of the lesson support the student in achieving the standards and goals. Moreover, the sequence of lesson 4 also supports the students in achieving the standards. Prior to doing any word problems, I explain to the student keywords associated with adding and subtracting. Also, I developed a poster with the keywords and plan to have that displayed during instruction. Taking this approach will allow the students to pay attention to keywords to solve the word problems.

QUESTION 2

Part A

The focus learner has been exposed to the concept of addition and subtraction. He has knowledge of the symbols associated with adding and subtracting. Based on the baseline data, the student does have little difficulty with addition and subtraction within 10s, but the issue is more of "silly" mistakes. The student is continuing to develop the knowledge for addition and subtraction to be quicker with basic math operations. The student is also learning to recognize words associated with adding and subtracting.

Part B

The student is able to express himself for his learning needs along with being able to communicate when he is struggling. The student does not show significant issues with impulse control, but rather is unable to stay focused for lengthy period of time. The student is aware that he is unable to stay focused and works on improving as there is a goal in his IEP. He has shown in past lessons that doing hands-on activities and in-class engagement supported him in staying focused. The focus learner is very talkative and social, and he does have friends that he interacts in class. When asked to work with others, he does not take any lead role, but does contribute minimally, which is likely due to him having several learning disabilities. In group settings, he does not have behavior issues that cause disruption.

Part C

My focus learner has been a foster child until recently when he was adopted. His adopted family is wealthy, giving him many outside resources for educational needs. His family pays for private math and reading tutoring to help with his disabilities. His adopted father is full time engineer while his mother is part-time music instructor. His mother is able to spend more time with him to help with homework and additional reading. The focus learner likes to play outside, play with toys, and write on walls. In particular, he likes to build structures with blocks. The focus learner is able to get along with all of the students. He has shown ability to be kind and giving, and he works well with his peers. The focus learner lacks organization skills as his papers are all over the place, which likely might be contributed to having a home maid. In addition to the family support, he is involved in local baseball team, which provides communication, friendship, and sportsmanship skills. Also, because he is recently adopted, social worker periodically does home visits.

Part D

Not applicable.

QUESTION 3

Part A

My focus learner needs to continue to learn the concept of counting, adding, and subtracting as his baseline data showed. These lessons will get him involved in prior knowledge along with new knowledge. In my lesson plans, I plan to have the focus learner engaged in-class discussions, which support my learner's need to remain focus during instruction. My focus learner is visual, so having everything written on the whiteboard supports his need and allows him to refer back to information. In each lesson, there are class activities that are completed that will allow me to see if the student is making progress; this will allow me to support any weak areas I see during instruction. The focus learner has no issues with other students and engages well, so in my lesson plans, I also use the students as a support system when faced with difficulty in answering questions. The student likes to write on the whiteboard, so in my lesson plans, I have activities where the student can come in front to work out the problems on the whiteboard. In addition, the focus learner likes to build structures with blocks, so I plan to use blocks in my lesson plans. One of the focus learner strength is getting along with classmates, so I make sure there will be ample interaction with peers during the learning segment.

Part B

In lesson one and two, I will have the student come up and attempt a practice problem after I show an example. This will allow the student to apply the knowledge learned. I will use scaffolding techniques by reviewing the concept of addition, then starting off with adding with two numbers, and then proceeding to adding with more than two numbers. Using this approach will challenge my learner to apply previous learned techniques (finger method, block method, and tally method). By having the student take on the role of the teacher in lesson three, I will challenge the learner to think about the process associated with doing the math problem as the student will be required to articulate the process to the other students. In lesson four, I will challenge the student by having him answer questions regarding the word problem to think about the process of solving; questions include:

- What is the question asking to find?
- What operation(s) are involved?
- What is/are the keyword(s) in the question?

In each of the lessons, I will have the student complete a worksheet, which will challenge the student on showing achievement of the objective(s) as the student is given what the expectations are in the beginning of the lesson.

Part C

My focus learner has a math disability. To ensure understanding and achievement of the learning goal, the lessons need to be structured to build on the final goal. The learning goal is to do word problems involving adding and subtracting within 20s. Instead of starting the learning segment with solving word problems, a lesson on adding will be completed, then subtracting, and then adding and subtracting together. Taking this approach will give my focus learner multiple opportunities to learn performing the operations. My focus learner is a visual learner, so I used different color blocks and markers. In addition, I will use a poster to support the student in learning the keywords associated with adding and subtracting. Because my focus learner is social and works well with peers, I will include group activities that will allow the students to provide feedback. The latter is supported by Lev Vygotsky's learning theory, which states that when students are learning new skill, they need an appropriate level of support to master skills. When students are given the appropriate level of support, they will eventually be able to complete skill independently. In the first two lessons, I will provide the support to my focus learner to complete each task. In the third lesson, I will step away from providing feedback and allowed peers to give feedback to one another. In lesson four, the student will complete final assessment independently to show understanding against learning objectives. In addition, Lev Vygotsky introduced social constructivism, in which social interaction with others assists the learner in putting meaning to information. Vygotsky noted a Zone of Proximal Development, in which learners can develop a certain level of meaning on their own but can grow even greater after interacting with classmates and instructors. Engaging with the instructor and working with classmates is planned throughout the learning segment.

Part D

Lesson 1

Generalization – I plan to have the students use what they learned from adding two numbers to the situation of adding more than two numbers.

Maintenance – I will have the students complete activities right after I teach them and at the conclusion of the lesson, which supports them in maintaining knowledge.

Self-directed – I will have the students grade their own worksheet. I will have them struggle to complete "11 + 4 =" with the finger method, allowing them to independently realize that it is not always the best approach.

Lesson 2

Generalization – I plan to have the students use what they learned from subtracting two numbers to the situation of subtracting more than two numbers.

Maintenance – I will have the students complete activities right after I teach them and at the conclusion of the lesson, which supports them in maintaining knowledge.

Self-directed – I will have the students grade their own worksheet. I also call on the students to support me in reaching the final answer to example problems during instruction.

Lesson 3

Generalization – Students will learn how to add within 20 in one lesson and then will learn how to subtract within 20 in another lesson. In lesson three, the students use that knowledge in different instances of adding and subtracting within 20s together.

Maintenance – I plan to let the students be the teachers in this lesson. As they struggle, they will be guided by peers. Struggle is a way to maintaining knowledge.

Self-directed – I will have the students grade their own worksheet. Students will be independently teaching their peers.

Lesson 4

Generalization – Students will use knowledge obtained from previous lessons to solve word problems.

Maintenance – I will let the students answer questions and guide me in achieving the right answers. As they struggle, they will be guided by myself or peers. Struggle is a way to maintaining knowledge.

Self-directed – In the beginning of the lesson, I will have students complete a pair activity. Two students will work out the problems using block method while the other two students work out the problems using tally method. The students will compare answers for grading purposes.

QUESTION 4

Part A

The communication skill that will be required is answering questions mainly through the concept of counting.

Part B

In all my instruction, I will be modeling example problems to support the student to understand the concept and process in solving and counting, which assist the student in answering questions related to counting. For example, in lesson one, I will show the students the object method, finger method, and tally method of adding two numbers. I will use the whiteboard to write an example problem and explain the process. Once I complete explaining, I will write a problem on the whiteboard for the students to answer. I will take the same approach when instructing to teach subtraction within 20s. During these lessons, I also will use blocks to engage the student. Modeling example problems and using blocks will support the focus learner in acquiring knowledge. In lesson one to four, I will give the students a worksheet to answer questions that require counting. By having the student answer example problems during instruction and answer questions on worksheets, the student will be able to maintain the skill of answering questions by counting.

Question 5

Part A

The baseline data includes assessment of the student on adding and subtracting within 10s along with few word problems that require operations within 10s. The daily assessment records require answering the following questions:

- Did the student participate when called upon?
- Did the student provide correct response majority of the time when asked questions?
- How many times was the student incorrect?
- Did the student engage with peers in learning?
- What score did the student receive on the lesson worksheet?

Documenting the incorrect response, observing the level of engagement, and grading the students' assignment provide evidence of the student learning and progressing toward the lesson objectives and the learning goal.

Documenting the participation, engagement, and accuracy of response will allow me to see if the supports provided during instruction are appropriate for my learner's need. The assessment also will allow me to see if the challenge is appropriate. If the student is constantly getting incorrect responses, perhaps the level of challenge is too much and adjustment is required.

Part B

In the first three lessons, I will have the focus learner complete worksheets, and I will give the student a red marker for self-grading purposes. I will go over each question and have the student correct himself on his paper. I will have the student write the number of incorrect questions on the top and collect papers for documentation purposes.

Task 2: Part A – Video Clips

The video summary is provided below for this edTPA® Special Education assessment portfolio.

- Instruction was done with four students.
- Instruction took place in a room at the library.
- A round table was in the center of the room with whiteboards on three of the four walls.
- Clip 1 included lesson 1 up to the completion of Step 5 (refer to instructional procedures section of the lesson plan).
- Clip 2 included lesson 4 up to the completion of Step 4 (refer to instructional procedures section of the lesson plan).

The remaining page is intentionally left blank.

Task 2: Part B – Instruction Commentary

QUESTION 1

The lesson plans that are included in the clip are the following:

- Clip 1 – Lesson 1
- Clip 2 – Lesson 4

The lesson plans were followed as written. No changes need to be documented.

QUESTION 2

Part A

Not applicable

Part B

The focus learner has a blue long-sleeve shirt in Clip 1, and the focus learner has a green sweater in Clip 2.

QUESTION 3

Part A

The following list ways I demonstrated respect and rapport with all learners:

- Required students to raise their hands if they wanted to speak and actually listen to their responses once I called on them. Also, I addressed the students with the first names, which shows them that I see them as individuals (Clip 1: timestamp 3:03).
- Tone used to communicate with the students was polite and clear to ensure the students followed directions. If the students were distracted, I redirected the students in a respectful manner to get them back on task. I used positive language to foster a safe learning environment where the students feel comfortable to express themselves and participate without being judged or imitated.(Clip 1: timestamp: 0:30, 1:43, 2:03, 4:23,7:30, and 8:30; Clip 2: timestamp: 1:23, 2:32, 4:32, 5:44, and 9:32).
- To establish a good learning relationship, I explained the importance of the lessons to the students, so they have understanding of why I was asking them to complete all the learning tasks. Students having understanding of the importance of tasks supported them in following directions. This is shown in the beginning of Clip 1 where I explain what we will be doing for lesson one, how it is connected to prior learning, and the reasons for learning to add within 20s (Clip 1: timestamp: 0:55).
- My focus learner has a math learning disability, so I made sure to give appropriate response time to him. This was done multiple times during the learning segment. In the video clip, I ask my focus learner to answer the question about the keywords associated in the word problem. He had to read the question again and took a minute to respond. I waited for him to respond (Clip 2: timestamp 8:32).

- I gave each student opportunities to participate and respond to the questions, so that they all can contribute and feel valued.

Part B

Below is a list with examples of how I provided a positive learning environment that both challenged and supported the focus learner.

- When students' were incorrect, I was not direct in letting them know they were incorrect. Instead, I encouraged them to make another attempt with a hint. If the second attempt was wrong, I explained background information and smoothly transitioned into giving the answer (Clip 1: timestamp: 4:12).
- I challenged the students by providing positive feedback and leading questions. For example, in lesson 4, when asked to solve the first word problem, I said "What is the question asking to find?" The student responded, but I asked the student "How did he know that is the answer?" (Clip 2: timestamp: 2:32). This ensures me that the student is not just guessing, but understanding the material presented.
- I also monitored, refocused, and redirected the students while working in pairs and groups along with assessing the students' ability to correctly complete the task. In lesson 1, I interacted with the focus learner and his partner as they were getting different answers. I encouraged them to work together to see which answers was correct (Clip 1: timestamp: 5:23).
- When the students were incorrect in the response provided to questions, I used positive reinforcement to encourage the student to continue with additional attempts. For example, when I asked the focus learner to solve the problem "4+6 =?", the focus learner incorrectly counted the blocks. I positively direct the focus learner to double check his work, and he was able to correct himself (Clip 1: timestamp: 3:12).

QUESTION 4

Part A

My strategies engaged and motivated the focus learner to develop learning. Those strategies included are outlined below.

- Using variety of methods in solving math problems; object method, tally method, and finger method. Giving the students multiple ways to learn motivates learners to select which method to use to solve the problems (Clip1 timestamp 2:03 – 4:39 – block method; Clip 1: timestamp: 4:55 – 7:33- tally method).
- I engaged the focus learner by showing a problem and then having him complete an example problem. By immediately having him work out a problem, the information learned is being applied and increases the chances of getting the correct answers, which encourages the student to continue to learn (Clip 1: timestamp: 3:23).
- Two of the students, one being the focus learner, are visual learners. As a result, I made sure to write all information on the whiteboard. I also included visual aids, such as posters.

- I also made sure the content and questions were at the right level of my focus learner. I did not want to put my focus learner in a struggling position to learn due to the lessons being outside of his current capabilities.

Part B

My focus learner has been exposed to adding and subtracting within 10s, so the lessons are a connection and extension to his prior knowledge. For example, when asked to explain the concept of addition and the symbol used, the focus learner was able to articulate the answer (Clip 1: timestamp: 1:31). My focus learner is visual and likes to write on walls/whiteboard, so I make sure to use the whiteboard as much as possible. In addition, I use visual aids (poster) in my instruction (Clip 2: timestamp: 1:44).

Part C

The following strategies were used to get the focus learner to become more independent and maintain active engagement.

- Direct instruction was used to show the block method, tally method, and finger method in solving adding and subtracting numbers (Clip 1: timestamp 1:30 - 3:20).
- With direct instruction, I use scaffolding approach. First, I started the student with adding/subtracting two numbers. Then, I built on that knowledge by going into adding/subtracting more than two numbers (Clip 1: timestamp 1:30 – 4:20).
- In each of my lessons, I had the students' complete worksheet at the end of the lesson, giving the students opportunity to show learning.
- I also have the focus learner complete example questions after I showed them how to do a problem (Clip 1: timestamp: 3:00; Clip 2: timestamp: 4:23). This allows the student to independently apply the knowledge. Taking this approach of having him apply the knowledge directly after instruction supports him in maintaining active engagement.
- Getting the student involved during instruction with leading questions allows the student to maintain active involvement (Clip 2: timestamp: 2:23).
- Another strategy used during the instruction was repetition. For example, I introduced addition and subtraction within 20 in lesson one and two, but I revisited both addition and subtraction together in lesson three. The repetition allowed the focus learner to maintain knowledge during the learning segment.

QUESTION 5

Part A

With the focus learner having multiple learning disabilities, I knew he could become easily unmotivated. To ensure his interest in the learning process, I had to make sure to highlight on his strengths. When the focus learner provided incorrect response, I provided positive feedback, and used tools, collaborative discussion, or whiteboard to elicit correct responses.

I provided wait time, repeated repetition, modeling, and hand signals to promote the application of learning. In my instruction, I use hand signals to point to the statements on the whiteboard to give hints to critical information. When the student gave a correct answer, I delivered positive feedback, such as saying "good job." Repetition was critical in my learning segment as the student was able to maintain and remember the knowledge associated with the learning goal. From doing multiple example problems, revisiting knowledge, multiple opportunities to practice, repetition is used throughout the learning segment. I provided adequate wait time to get a response from the focus student. If he was having a difficult time verbalizing his response, I intervened to support him. Additionally, I provided my focus learner with concrete feedback when he was on the right approach and when he was on the wrong approach.

Part B

In lesson 1, I give the student feedback on the example problem he completed during instruction "4+6 =". I redirected him to count the number of blocks by encouraging him to double check his work (Clip 1: timestamp: 3:12). He was able to apply that when completing the worksheet as I observed him checking his answer twice. The feedback provided in lesson one was used in lesson 4 when completing the final worksheet (as he made crossed his work and redid it). In each of the lessons, I included a worksheet to complete that gives the student opportunity to apply feedback given related to the learning goal.

Part C

The following shows my action to get the focus learner to self-evaluate and self-correct to improve performance:

- In each lesson, I had the focus learner complete a worksheet. Once completed, I gave the students a red marker for self-grading purposes. I went over each question and had the focus learner correct himself on his paper.
- Encouraging my focus learner to double check allowed him the opportunity to self-correct. For example, when I asked the focus learner to solve the problem "4+6 =?", the focus learner incorrectly counted the blocks. I encouraged him to double check his work, and he was able to correct himself (Clip 1: timestamp: 3:12).
- In lesson one, I interacted with the focus learner and his partner as they were getting different answers. I encouraged them to work together to see which answers were correct (Clip 1: timestamp: 5:23). This gave them the opportunity to evaluate themselves and make necessary corrections.

QUESTION 6

Part A

The content of the lessons are a reflection of my learner's development stage, age, strengths, and needs. The lessons do not include a lot of information to process as my focus learner has reading and math disability. To ensure the focus learner is acquiring mathematical knowledge, very little reading skills are required. In lesson four, the word problems used are simple to allow the student to focus on the math concepts. This approach allowed the student to actively participate in the class discussion as he was not struggling with the reading (Clip 2: timestamp: 6:32).

Each of the lessons is connected to the succeeding lesson, so that the focus learner is gradually learning the content he needs to meet the learning goal. The focus learner was supported by gestural prompts, verbal prompts, and repetition. For example, when I asked the focus learner to solve the problem "4+6 =?", the focus learner incorrectly counted the blocks. I encouraged him to double check his work, and he was able to correct himself (Clip 1: timestamp: 3:12). Example of repetition is shown throughout the learning segment. I showed the focus learner how to complete a problem, have the student complete a similar problem, and then assessed the student on similar problem in worksheet (modeling shown in Clip 1: timestamp: 3:30).

The instructional strategies that supported the focus learner's progress toward the lesson objectives were modeling, scaffolding, and repetition. I modeled answering example questions (Clip 1: timestamp: 3:30). The activities were scaffold throughout the learning segment to the provide focus learner with the necessary support he needed to achieve the learning objectives. For example, I started off in lesson one showing how to add two numbers (Clip 1: timestamp: 2:30-4:00) and then proceeded into modeling how to complete addition with more than three numbers. Repetition was a strategy used to ensure understanding of the objectives, and repetition supported my focus learners need. Having modeled a problem, engaging the student in completing similar example problems, and completing worksheets related to the problems are examples of repetition. With my focus learner having a math learning disability, repetition was critical in progressing the learner toward the lesson objectives. Repetition and modeling is required for the learner to maintain knowledge.

Part B

In lesson one and two, I modeled doing example problems and had the focus learner complete example problems. In lesson three, I had the focus learner take on the role of the teacher, and he was to complete math problems that involved adding and subtracting together. Because the focus learner was responsible for teaching, the focus learner had to think deeper in explaining how to complete the problem. In lesson four, I used a poster to show the students the keywords associated with adding and subtracting. This poster was displayed throughout the lesson. As the focus learner engaged in class discussion and activities, the focus learner used the poster to self-direct himself. Also, when the focus learner got a question incorrect, I always gave opportunity for the learner to correct himself.

QUESTION 7

Part A

The following are changes I recommend to better support or extend the student's performance:

- Instead of directly going into showing how to add more than two numbers, the better approach might be to challenge the student to explain how to approach adding numbers with more than two numbers.

- In lesson one, I place 9 block squares and 3 red block squares. The best approach might be to have the focus learner initiate the process.
- In my video, I had all the students count the number of blocks or tallies when working together. Better approach might be to have one student count.
- Include a video in one of the lessons. For example, showing a video on how to use the block method or finger method. Or, include a game in one of the lesson plans.

Part B

- Giving the students the opportunity to challenge themselves is critical to expanding thinking skills, which is why I recommend challenging the student to explain how to approach adding numbers with more than two numbers. This gives the student opportunity to generalize on previous information learned.
- Having the student initiate the process of putting block together can trigger the next step without intervention. Having the student place 9 square blocks and 3 red square blocks on the table can be a way for the student to self-direct learning.
- Having all the students count together caused confusion, so to ensure organization best approach is to have one student count.
- These lessons can include additional different activities to make the learning segment more involved. Differentiation is key to meeting the students needs and progressing student learning, which is supported by Carol Ann Tomlinson. Differentiation can be in content, processes, the learning environment, and assessments. Differentiation is a way for teachers to respond to students' learning needs. With my focus learner being visual a video or game is a good way to provide differentiation at the same time support his learning style.

Task 3: Part A – Work Sample

Student Name

Final Assessment

Directions: Answer the follow questions.

QUESTION 1

Solve the following problem using the block method:

11 + 9 =

18

20

QUESTION 2

Solve the following problem using the block method:

15 - 3 =

12

QUESTION 3

Solve the following problem using the block method:

14 - 2 + 3 =

12

13

12

15

QUESTION 4

Solve the following problem using your fingers:

5 + 17 - 5 =

QUESTION 5

Name three keywords associated with adding.

add
total
sum

QUESTION 6

Martin has 17 coins. He gave 3 to Mary and 2 to Derrick. Derrick gave back 1 of his cards to Martin. How many total cards does Martin have left?

17 - 3 - 2 + 1

13

QUESTION 7

Name 3 keywords associated with subtracting.

minus
subtract

QUESTION 8

Kathy has 4 apples, 2 strawberries, and 7 blueberries. How many fruits in total does Kathy have?

$4 + 2 + 7$

13

QUESTION 9

There are 19 books in the classroom, 4 students take the book home, and 2 do not return the books at the end of the school year. How many books are there in the classroom at the end of the school year?

$19 \ 4 \ 2$

QUESTION 10

Victor brought 18 flowers. He gave 2 to his mother and 2 to his sister. Victor also gave 3 flowers to his teacher. How many flowers does Victor have left?

$18 - 2 - 2 - 3$

11

Student Name: ████

Daily Assessment Record

LESSON NUMBER: |

OBJECTIVE:

The objective of the lesson is to gain knowledge of adding within 20.

QUESTION 1

Did the student participate when called upon?

Yes - No issues here.

QUESTION 2

Did the student provide correct response majority of the time when asked questions?

Yes - One instance student was incorrect, but corrected himself

QUESTION 3

Did the student engage with peers in learning?

Yes - No issues here

QUESTION 4

What score did the student receive on the lesson worksheet?

70%

QUESTION 5

Did the student show overall achievement of the learning objective(s)?

Yes

Student Name: ████

Daily Assessment Record

LESSON NUMBER: 2

OBJECTIVE:

The objective of the lesson is to gain knowledge of subtracting within 20

QUESTION 1

Did the student participate when called upon?

Yes - No issues here

QUESTION 2

Did the student provide correct response majority of the time when asked questions?

Yes - No issues here

QUESTION 3

Did the student engage with peers in learning?

Yes - No issues here.

QUESTION 4

What score did the student receive on the lesson worksheet?

80%

QUESTION 5

Did the student show overall achievement of the learning objective(s)?

Yes

Student Name:

Daily Assessment Record

LESSON NUMBER: 3

OBJECTIVE:

The objective of the lesson is to gain knowledge of adding and subtracting within 20.

QUESTION 1

Did the student participate when called upon?

Yes- No issues here

QUESTION 2

Did the student provide correct response majority of the time when asked questions?

Yes-No issues here

QUESTION 3

Did the student engage with peers in learning?

Yes - No issues hone

QUESTION 4

What score did the student receive on the lesson worksheet?

80%

QUESTION 5

Did the student show overall achievement of the learning objective(s)?

Yes

Student Name:

Daily Assessment Record

LESSON NUMBER: 4

OBJECTIVE:

The objective of the lesson is to solve basic word problems involving addition, subtraction, or addition and subtracting together within 20.

QUESTION 1

Did the student participate when called upon?

Yes - No issues here

QUESTION 2

Did the student provide correct response majority of the time when asked questions?

Yes - No issues here

QUESTION 3

Did the student engage with peers in learning?

Yes - No issues here

QUESTION 4

What score did the student receive on the lesson worksheet?

87%

QUESTION 5

Did the student show overall achievement of the learning objective(s)?

Yes

Student Name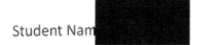

Pre-Assessment

Directions: Answer the follow questions.

QUESTION 1

Solve the following problem:

5 + 3 =

8

Good job, remember to always check your work!!!

QUESTION 2

Solve the following problem:

5 - 3 =

2

QUESTION 3

Circle ALL words associated with subtracting.

(left)   (minus)   sum   (take away)   in all   (less)

QUESTION 4

Solve the following problem:

7 - 5 =

2

QUESTION 5

Solve the following problem:

9 - 3 =

6

QUESTION 6

Solve the following problem:

1 + 3 + 3 =

7

QUESTION 7

Solve the following problem:

5 + 4 - 3 =

8   4

$$5 + 4 - 3$$
$$9 - 3$$
$$6$$

92

Task 3: Part C – Evidence of Feedback

87%

Student Name ████████

Super Work!!!
keep it up!!!

Final Assessment

Directions: Answer the follow questions.

QUESTION 1

Solve the following problem using the block method:

$11 + 9 =$

18
20

QUESTION 2

Solve the following problem using the block method:

$15 - 3 =$

12

QUESTION 3

Solve the following problem using the block method:

$14 - 2 + 3 =$

12
13

✓ QUESTION 4

Solve the following problem using your fingers:

5 + 17 - 5 =

17

✓ QUESTION 5

Name three keywords associated with adding.

add

total   Good Job!!!

SUM

✓ QUESTION 6

Martin has 17 coins. He gave 3 to Mary and 2 to Derrick. Derrick gave back 1 of his cards to Martin. How many total cards does Martin have left?

17 - 3 - 2 + 1   Good job underlining!!!

13

X QUESTION 7 (7 points given)

Name 3 keywords associated with subtracting.

minus

✓ subtract

left or give or less

94

QUESTION 8

Kathy has 4 apples, 2 strawberries, and 7 blueberries. How many fruits in total does Kathy have?

$$4 + 2 + 7$$
$$13$$

QUESTION 9

There are 19 books in the classroom, 4 students take the book home, and 2 do not return the books at the end of the school year. How many books are there in the classroom at the end of the school year?

$$19 + 4 - 2 = 13$$

QUESTION 10

Victor brought 18 flowers. He gave 2 to his mother and 2 to his sister. Victor also gave 3 flowers to his teacher. How many flowers does Victor have left?

$$18 - 2 - 2 - 3$$
$$11$$

Task 4: Part D – Assessment Commentary

QUESTION 1 – Analyzing the Focus Learner Performance

Part A

The objectives measured in each of the daily assessment records are:

- Lesson 1 - The objective of the lesson is to gain knowledge of adding within 20.
- Lesson 2 - The objective of the lesson is to gain knowledge of subtracting within 20
- Lesson 3 - The objective of the lesson is to gain knowledge of adding and subtracting within 20.
- Lesson 4 - The objective of the lesson is to solve basic word problems involving addition, subtraction, or addition and subtracting together within 20.

Part B

No changes made that require documentation.

Part C

Sample work is the student's final assessment from Lesson 4.

Part D

The following table shows the focus learner's progress on the worksheets completed in the learning segment.

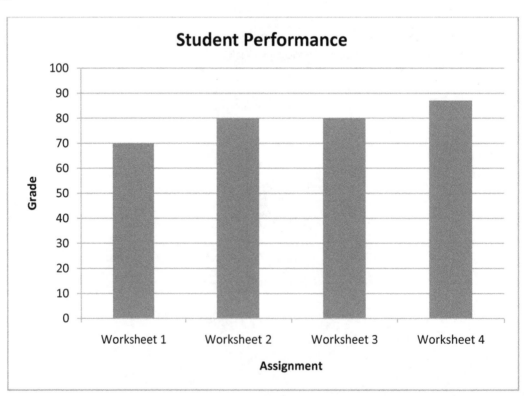

Baseline Data Summary

The baseline data collected demonstrated the student's level of prerequisite knowledge from the learning segments. The assessment collected highlights the student's strengths and weaknesses in regards to the content. The student is able to do addition and subtraction within 10s. He did make one mistake in the pre-assessment on math calculation. He did struggle with identifying words associated with subtraction.

Part E

The focus learner does understand the information presented during the lesson, as he is able to complete in-class example problems with moderate support. The student also has demonstrated passing score on worksheets for each of the lesson. The focus learner did not get any of the problems incorrect that required him to use the block method. In addition, during the final assessment, he desired to use the blocks most of the time. During instruction, when the student rushed to complete a problem, he made a mistake. When he did not use any of the methods presented, he made a mistake. He needs to continue to apply the methods used in solving problems, especially at this early stage of learning. Moreover, none of the errors made during in-class participation or worksheets were consistent, which indicates there is no major gap in content. Also, the focus learner has to read word problems multiple times and takes time to process information, indicating he has some difficulty, which is not a surprised due to his reading disability.

Part F

Showing example problems in class and having the focus learner work examples immediately afterwards provided the focus learner immediate opportunity to apply knowledge. This contributed in him understanding and performing well on the worksheets. Scaffolding was used during instruction, which contributed in him processing the information better. Lesson one was only on addition, and lesson two was only on subtraction. Lesson three combined both addition and subtraction, and as I observed the student, he did not need as much support. His learning progress for the objectives of the learning segment is shown on the final assessment in which he received an 87% out of 100%; good improvement from baseline data assessment. Using the whiteboard and blocks contributed in getting the student engaged in doing the example problems, which supported his learning. According to the daily assessment records, engagement was not an issue in any of the lessons.

QUESTION 2 – Feedback to Guide Further Learning

Part A

Evidence of feedback was provided on the students work sample document.

Part B

During instruction, I informed my focus learner to check his work and try again. I also encouraged him to double check his work (indicated in the baseline data assessment as well). This error prevention method supported the student in performing well on the learning goal as in the final assessment for question one and three, the student made mistake but corrected himself. During instruction, I provided the leaner with clear, simple, and direct feedback. The focus learner responds to positive feedback, so I made sure to comment on the areas that he did well. For example, in the final assessment, I wrote "Super Work!!! Keep It Up!!!" Because my focus learner is visual, I used check marks for correct answers and crosses for incorrect answers. Moreover, I corrected the student's work when he was incorrect; for example, questions seven and nine on the final assessment. The focus learner needs to continue to work on operations within 20s to ensure learning is maintained, but also needs to continue with addition of higher numbers. As a result, the positive feedback provides encouragement to continue with the learning process.

Part C

During instruction, I gave my focus learner feedback verbally. To ensure the feedback was being received and understood, I asked the student if he understood what I stated. At times, I asked the student to repeat the feedback. Activities and example problems from the instruction were related to the end of lesson worksheet. The student's performance on the worksheets provides indication if the student understood and used the feedback. As shown in the table above, the student performed well on the worksheets.

I provided the focus learner with positive feedback throughout the learning segment to let him know what he was doing correctly. When the focus learner was struggling, I provided support to guide his understanding. One of the main feedbacks during instruction was to re-check math work. The student used the feedback in the final assessment, and rechecking work will be relevant in future tasks of addition/subtraction. The corrections guide the student towards improving upon his mistakes for subsequent learning. Re-checking work does not simply apply to math, but can be extended to other academic subject areas.

The student performed acceptable on the final assessment with minor mistakes. Therefore, the best way for the focus learner to apply the feedback from final assessment is to have subsequent assignments focusing more on questions that target concepts the student did not receive full credit.

QUESTION 3 – Evidence of Use of the Expressive/Receptive Communication Skill

Part A

The communication skill required to participate in the learning tasks and demonstrate learning was to answer questions through the concept of counting.

Part B

Expressive Communication

Planned supports for expressive communication included using whiteboard, paired activities, modeling, and worksheets. The focus learner used the whiteboard to communicate his answers to the class. For example, in lesson one, I the focus learner came up to the board and completed the problem "4 + 6 =" (Clip 1: timestamp 3:40). In addition, in lesson three, the focus learner used the whiteboard to teach math problems as he took the role as the teacher. The focus learner strength is interacting with peers, so I included activities that allowed them to communicate with his classmates, which engaged the learner and supported him to demonstrate learning. The focus learner has a math learning disability, so he needs to be shown how to do problems in multiple ways to be successful. Using modeling allowed me to show the student how to complete math problems, but also engage him in the process (Clip 1: timestamp: 2:33). In the process of modeling problems, I used repetition as a way to get the student exposed multiple times to the concept being taught. In addition, my instruction involved using multiple methods of adding (block method, finger method, and tally method). Completing the worksheets in each lesson allowed the student to express his answers to questions. The performance on the worksheets indicated demonstration of the learning goal.

Part C

Repetition allowed the student to practice similar math problems multiple times. In addition, the final assessment (Task 3 Part A) included questions from all the objectives. In taking this approach, the student became adapted to answer similar types of questions and allowed the focus learner to maintain the communication skill of answer questions through counting. Being able to add/subtract and count are critical aspects of individual at an early age. By developing the ability to count, add, and subtract, the student generalize adding and subtracting in other instances, such as counting days of weeks or counting money. Repetition is a critical element in my lesson plans as repetition allowed the focus student to review and practice the concept being presented in the lesson.

QUESTION 4 – Using Assessment to Inform Instruction

Part A

The focus learner needs to continue to do more practice in adding and subtracting within 20s to be able to do these operations quicker. Having the focus learner complete different types of activities, such as games or group activities, will allow the learner to apply knowledge learned. As mention earlier, Carol Ann Tomlinson research supports differentiation in process and content to support the students learning needs. In addition, the student does need to focus on word problems. The student showed some difficulty in completing word problems, so the best approach might be to devote a re-enforcement lesson on word problems associated with adding/subtracting. In the final assessment, the word problem that was the longest, the student had difficulty answering. A re-enforcement lesson on breaking down longer worded problems supports the cognitivism learning theory, which is suited well for problem solving, where the concepts are complex and must be broken down into smaller parts. Ideas and concepts from these problems are linked to prior knowledge, which in turn helps the learner develop a stronger comprehension. Once mastery of adding/subtracting within 20s, the focus learner can move onto adding/subtracting with higher numbers and with other methods (ex. carry over).

Part B

No major implications or changes are required in the students IEP goals/curriculum. Only documentation is required that states the student has perform acceptable in counting within 20s. Student needs to continue to practice adding/subtracting and completing word problems within 20s and move forward with higher numbers.

Special Education Score and Evaluation Analysis

The Special Education edTPA® portfolio received a score of 44. With edTPA® being subjective exam, the score can be in the range of 42-46 depending on the grader. The lesson topic is based on basic concept of adding and subtracting, likely resulting in the use of simple supports and instructional strategies. In most States and university programs, this edTPA® portfolio is considered passing.

Below is a table that breaks down the scores for each of the rubrics. The rubric numbers are referenced only, so candidates are recommended to refer to the Special Education edTPA® handbook for rubric details.

Rubric	Score	Comments/Analysis
1	4	The candidate included individual education program, standards, lesson objectives, and planned supports. The objectives, materials, and planned supports were sequenced to move the focus student in achieving the learning goal. The worksheets associated with the lessons targeted the objectives, and the worksheets were measurable outcomes.
2	3	The instructional tasks were at the right level for the focus learner. The candidate mentioned that the student desired to use blocks to build structures. However, to receive higher score, the candidate needed to establish a stronger connection of tasks/supports to the student's strengths, needs, and interests.
3	2	The candidate needed to mention how instruction and planned supports were used to support the student in learning despite of his learning disability. The research and theory justification was weak. The candidate needed to provide additional theory along with more details.
4	3	The planned supports indicated in the portfolio were general. To obtain additional points, candidate needed to include more specific planned support.
5	3	The candidate included baseline data and daily assessment records aligned to the lesson objectives and provided evidence for monitoring progress. To increase the score, the candidate needed to include assessments that give challenge and support in regards to the learner's strengths and weaknesses.
6	4	Throughout the video, the candidate showed respect and rapport to all students. The candidate explained this well in the commentary.
7	2	The video does not show a strong connection to student's prior learning and new learning. The candidate used general strategies for engaging the student. To obtain higher score, the candidate needed to include creative strategies and establish stronger connection to personal and cultural assets.
8	3	Candidate does engage the student in trying again and giving clues to get the student in the right direction. The candidate does give opportunity for the student to apply feedback. The candidate could have allowed the student to initiate responses.
9	3	Candidate used the instructional strategies (repetition, modeling, and scaffolding). There was no evidence indicating that the candidate used instructional strategies to capitalize on the student's strengths.

10	3	Candidate included the changes and reasons for the changes. Justification was connected to the learner's need and research/theory, but the information indicated was general. Providing detail, concrete information could increase the score.
11	2	The analysis focused more on the accomplishment of the objectives and no detail information connecting to strengths, planned supports, or error prevention strategies.
12	3	The feedback provided was more focused on the learner's strength. To increase score, the candidate needed to relate feedback to the learner's need.
13	3	Feedback was provided to the student, but opportunities did not exist that allowed the learner to use the feedback related to strengths or needs in connection to the learning goal. To increase the score, the candidate could provide more opportunities to apply feedback and support the student in using the feedback.
14	3	The candidate did a good job explaining the use of communication skills to the learning tasks. Details on how planned supports assisted in the use of communication skill could have increased the score.
15	3	The next steps of instruction were general. The connection to research and theories was also general.
Total Score	44	This edTPA® portfolio is considered passing. The candidate showed planning of lessons targeting the focus learner. Instruction was conducted and aligned with basic requirements of edTPA®. Assessments were provided that tracked the focus learner's progress toward the learning goal. Commentary responses were written at an acceptable level (not mastery level).

This page is intentionally left blank.

Chapter 15 - Elementary Education Literacy edTPA®

The Elementary Education – Literacy edTPA® requires the candidates to identify the central focus that includes essential literacy strategies and use of related skills. The candidates will identify one central focus and develop 3-5 consecutive learning experiences (lesson plans).

The goal of the Elementary Education – Literacy edTPA® is for the candidates to demonstrate ability to plan, instruct, and assess elementary students. This chapter includes a complete edTPA® portfolio for the Elementary Education – Literacy subject area.

This chapter covers the following:

- Task 1: Part A – Literacy Context for Learning Information
- Task 1: Part B – Lesson Plans for Learning Segment
- Task 1: Part C – Instructional Material
- Task 1: Part D – Literacy Assessments
- Task 1: Part E – Literacy Planning Commentary
- Task 2: Part A – Video Clips
- Task 2: Part B – Literacy Instruction Commentary
- Task 3: Part A – Student Literacy Work Samples
- Task 3: Part B – Evidence of Feedback
- Task 3: Part C – Literacy Assessment Commentary
- Task 3: Part D – Evaluation Criteria
- Evaluation Analysis

edTPA® Example and Reference Note

In this chapter, an example Elementary Education - Literacy edTPA® is included with a group of third grade students. The portfolio is an unedited example, so the portfolio does include grammar, punctuation, and usage errors. All documents that are submitted for the real edTPA® submission are included except for the video. Instead, summary of the video is provided.

NOTE: Due to copyright laws, the handbook does not use direct wording/questions from the edTPA® handbook. Templates (and wording) provided by SCALE will not be used and direct content/questions from templates and commentaries are not used. Candidates are recommended to have a copy of the assessment handbook when reviewing this chapter.

Task 1 Part A – Elementary Literacy Context for Learning Information

About the School Where You Are Teaching

Question 1: Document the type of school and location.

Elementary School; Urban

Question 2: Document any special features of the school or classroom that impact teaching.

No information necessary to document.

Question 3: Document any school/district requirements or expectations that might affect planning or delivery of instruction.

No information necessary to document.

About the Class Featured for the edTPA®

Question 1: How much time is devoted for literacy instruction in the classroom?

Typically, 90-120 minutes are devoted to literacy/language instruction per day. Rarely does instruction exceed 120 minutes.

Question 2: Is there any ability grouping or tracking that might impact the class?

No, ability grouping.

Question 3: Document textbooks used for literacy/language instruction.

No textbooks used for this literacy/language instruction.

Question 4: List additional resources for literacy/language instruction.

Additional resources include SmartBoard, posters, jeopardy game (requiring computer), and teacher developed reading articles.

About the Students In the Classroom

Question 1: Document the grade level or levels.

The classroom is a group of third graders.

Question 2: Document the number of students.

There are total 6 students; 4 boys and 2 girls.

Question 3: Complete the total below.

Students with IEPs/504 Plans

IEPs/504 Plans Needs	Number of Students	Supports/Accommodations/Modifications
Mild Speech Disorder	1* (also identified as struggling reader)	Receives speech services (once a week for 30 mins) Spelling and reading are modified
Visual processing	1	Preferential seating, worksheets with larger print, close monitoring

Student with Other Learning Needs

Learning Needs	Number of Students	Supports/Accommodations/Modifications
Struggling readers	1*(also identified as having mild speech disorder)	Appropriate text level, guided reading, ongoing reading assessments (running records), double dosing of guided reading groups with another teacher.
ELL	2	English learners with ESL teacher, guided reading groups, guided writing groups, visual cues, and guided notes,

Task 1 – Part B – Lesson Plans for Learning Segment

Learning Experience One

Topic/Title: Nouns and Pronouns

Level: 3rd Grade Instruction

Central Focus

The central focus is for the students to understand, recognize, and use nouns, pronouns, verbs, adjectives, and adverbs when reading and writing.

Educational Standards

CCSS.ELA-Literacy.L.3.1 - Demonstrate command of the conventions of standard English grammar and usage when writing or speaking.

CCSS.ELA-Literacy.L.3.1.a - Explain the function of nouns, pronouns, verbs, adjectives, and adverbs in general and their functions in particular sentences.

Objective(s)

The following are objectives associated with this lesson:

- understand the function of nouns and pronouns

- identify nouns and pronouns in sentences

- write sentences using nouns and pronouns

Instructional Procedures (step by step instructional procedures)

Note: Students are sitting on the carpet.

Step 1: I will welcome the students to the classroom and inform them that we have an exciting lesson planned. I will explain we will be learning about the key parts of speech of sentences (nouns and pronouns). Moreover, I will explain the big picture/central focus along with how this lesson connects to the central focus.

Step 2: To engage the students, I will have the students complete a think-pair-share activity by asking them what comes to mind with the words noun and pronoun. Students will be given a worksheet to document their thoughts. This allows the students to show pre-existing knowledge.

Step 3: All students will be filling in a KWL chart. To promote the students active involvement, I will ask the following questions:

- What is a noun?

- What is a pronoun?

- What do you want to know about noun?

- What do you want to know about pronouns?

Step 4: Using the SMART Board, I will display the slide for teaching nouns. I will explain to the students the function of the element and how the element can be incorporated in sentences. I will also provide suggestions on how to determine the element in sentences.

Step 5: I will also show sentence(s) or paragraph(s), and I will ask the students to find the noun(s) and will ask for their reasoning.

Step 6: I will continue Step 4 and Step 5 for pronoun.

Step 7: To reinforce the learning, I will show two posters with sentences in large font, and I will ask students to identify the pronouns/nouns. On the back of the posters, I will have the answer written with a picture.

Step 8: I will do an in-class activity with the students. I will have six index cards: three cards with nouns and three cards with pronouns. The index cards will be in a brown paper bag. I will have the students pick one card.

Step 9: The students will be asked to think of a sentence using the part of speech written on the index cards, and the students will be asked to write the sentence on the SMART Board. The student will be asked to identify what element was used and where it is in the sentence. I will also model a sentence on the whiteboard for the students.

Closure Procedures

Students will complete a worksheet to demonstrate learning of the objectives. As the students complete the worksheet independently, I will walk around the classroom to ensure the students are actively working.

Once the worksheet is completed, the class will go over the correct answers together. I will give the students a red marker to self grade.

To conclude the lesson, I will summarize the activities and give insight into the next activity.

Assessment(s)

Pre-assessment will be completed using the KWL chart. Students will document what they know and what they want to know.

I will be informally assessing the students when I ask them to write a sentence on the SMART Board.

At the end of the lesson, a formal assessment will be conducted to test students' knowledge on nouns and pronouns.

Academic Language – Language Function

Students will be asked to identify nouns and pronouns.

Academic Language – Language Vocabulary

The following are vocabulary words: nouns and pronouns.

Academic Language – Language Demand

The academic language demands the students will be using to participate in the tasks are writing and listening. Students will be asked to listen as I instruct the class. Students will be asked to write a sentence on the SMART Board. Students will be given a KWL worksheet to document information they know and what want to learn. During think-pair-share, the students will be given worksheet to document their thoughts.

Instructional Resources

None

Instructional Materials

The following are material used during the instruction:

- SMART Board

- KWL Chart (worksheets)

- Instructional Worksheets

- Index cards

- Posters

Instructional Environment – Modifications/Adaptations

The instruction is planned to allow the students with various learning modes to participate. Modes include group/partner activities, independent work, visualize pictures/information, and written assignments.

Students will start the lesson by setting on the carpet, but when completing the worksheets, the students will be instructed to go back to their desks. This change will allow the students who have difficulty sitting/focusing in one spot for long time to refocus.

Appropriate font will be used on SMART Board and worksheets to allow individuals with difficulty in reading/writing small print. This will support one student with 504 plan for visual processing along with visual learners.

Learning Experience Two

Topic/Title: Identify Nouns and Pronouns

Level: 3rd Grade Instruction

Central Focus

The central focus is for the students to understand, recognize, and use nouns, pronouns, verbs, adjectives, and adverbs when reading and writing.

Educational Standards

CCSS.ELA-Literacy.L.3.1 - Demonstrate command of the conventions of standard English grammar and usage when writing or speaking.

CCSS.ELA-Literacy.L.3.1.a - Explain the function of nouns, pronouns, verbs, adjectives, and adverbs in general and their functions in particular sentences.

CCSS.ELA-Literacy.RI.3.1 - Ask and answer questions to demonstrate understanding of a text, referring explicitly to the text as the basis for the answers.

Objective(s)

The following are objectives associated with this lesson:

- read third grade level reading articles and recognize nouns and pronouns

- explain the use of nouns and pronouns

- use nouns and pronouns to support in asking/answering questions related to the reading articles

Instructional Procedures (step by step instructional procedures)

Note: Students are at the round table.

Step 1: I will welcome the students to the classroom and inform them that we have an exciting lesson planned. I will explain we will be reading a third grade reading article and identifying nouns and pronouns along with answering comprehension questions. Moreover, I will explain the big picture/central focus along with how this lesson connects to the central focus.

Step 2: To engage the students and activate prior knowledge, I will have the students complete a think-pair-share activity by giving them a worksheet on nouns and pronouns. I will select students to share the answers they obtained with their partner.

Step 3: I will give each student a copy of the reading article. I will explain to the students we will read together by taking turns. Once we finish reading one paragraph, we will stop reading to underline the nouns and pronouns. Students will be asked to complete this on their own copy. Once completed, I will ask students to inform me what they identified, and I will document it on the SMART Board. Before moving forward, I will make sure that all nouns and pronouns have been identified.

Step 4: I will ask students comprehension questions regarding the paragraph. The students will be asked to provide the answer, but also explain how nouns and pronouns supported them in answering the questions.

Step 5: We will complete step three and four for each paragraph in the reading article.

Step 6: Next, the students will do a similar activity in groups of three. The students will be given a short reading article for which they will have to identify all the nouns and pronouns and answer comprehension questions.

Step 7: Once completed, the group will select one student to share the answers to the class.

Closure Procedures

Students will be asked to write one paragraph about a sport they have played. Then, the students will exchange their paper. Students will be asked to underline all nouns and pronouns. Once completed, the paper will be returned to the original writer, who will check to see if all nouns/pronouns have been underlined. I will then do a final check and provide feedback on the students' paper.

To conclude the lesson, I will summarize the activities and give insight into the next activity.

Assessment(s)

I will be informally assessing the students when reading together, identifying nouns and pronouns and answering questions (Step 4 and 5).

I will grade the students worksheet that they complete in groups (Step 6 and 7).

At the end of the lesson, a formal assessment will be conducted to test students' knowledge on nouns and pronouns.

Academic Language – Language Function

Students will be asked to identify nouns and pronouns along with identify details of passage to answer comprehension questions.

Academic Language – Language Vocabulary

The following are vocabulary words: noun and pronoun.

Academic Language – Language Demand

The academic language demands the students will be using to participate in the tasks are writing, reading, and listening. Students will be asked to listen to myself and other students while reading. Students will be asked to underline nouns, pronouns, verbs, adjectives, and adverbs, and answer comprehension questions.

Instructional Resources

None

Instructional Materials

The following are material used during the instruction:

- SMART Board

- KWL Chart (worksheets)

- Instructional Worksheets

- Reading articles

Instructional Environment – Modifications/Adaptations

The instruction is planned to allow the students with various learning modes to participate. Modes include group/partner activities, independent work, visualize pictures/information, and written assignments.

Appropriate font will be used on SMART Board and worksheets to allow individuals with difficulty in reading/writing small print. This will support one student with 504 plan for visual processing along with visual learners.

Learning Experience Three

Topic/Title: Verbs, Adjectives, and Adverbs

Level: 3rd Grade Instruction

Central Focus

The central focus is for the students to understand, recognize, and use nouns, pronouns, verbs, adjectives, and adverbs when reading and writing.

Educational Standards

CCSS.ELA-Literacy.L.3.1 - Demonstrate command of the conventions of standard English grammar and usage when writing or speaking.

CCSS.ELA-Literacy.L.3.1.a - Explain the function of nouns, pronouns, verbs, adjectives, and adverbs in general and their functions in particular sentences.

Objective(s)

The following are objectives associated with this lesson:

- understand the function of verbs, adjectives, and adverbs

- identify verbs, adjectives, and adverbs in sentences

- write sentences using verbs, adjectives, and adverbs

Instructional Procedures (step by step instructional procedures)

Note: Students are sitting on the carpet.

Step 1: I will welcome the students to the classroom and inform them that we have an exciting lesson planned. I will explain we will be learning about verbs, adjectives, and adverbs. Moreover, I will explain the big picture/central focus along with how this lesson connects to the central focus.

Step 2: To engage the students, I will have the students complete a think-pair-share activity by asking them what comes to mind with the words verb, adjective, and adverb. Students will be given a worksheet to document their thoughts. This allows the students to show pre-existing knowledge.

Step 3: All students will fill in a KWL chart. To promote the students active involvement, I will ask the following questions:

- What is a verb?

- What is adverb?

- What do you want to know about adjective?

Step 4: Using the SMART Board, I will display the slide for verbs. I will explain to the student the function of verbs and how verbs can be incorporated into sentences. I will also provide suggestions on how to determine the verbs in sentences.

Step 5: I will also show sentence(s) or paragraph(s), and I will ask students to find the verbs and explain why they selected the answer.

Step 6: I will continue Step 4 and Step 5 for adverbs and adjectives.

Step 7: To reinforce the learning, I will show two posters with sentences in large font, and I will ask students to identify the elements. On the back of the posters, I will have the answer written with a picture.

Step 8: I will do an in-class jeopardy game with the students on all the terms (nouns, pronouns, verbs, adverbs, and adjectives). I will use online website to present the jeopardy game. Students will be asked to raise hands to be called on, and I will navigate the web tool. The students will be informed that the top three winners will receive a candy bar.

Closure Procedures

Students will complete a worksheet to demonstrate learning of the objectives. As the students complete the worksheet independently, I will walk around the classroom to ensure the students are actively working.

Once the worksheet is completed, we will go over the correct answers together. I will give the students a red marker to self grade.

To conclude the lesson, I will summarize the activities and give insight into the next activity.

Assessment(s)

Pre-assessment will be completed using the KWL chart. Students will document what they know and what they want to know.

During the jeopardy game, I will be informally assessing the students performance.

A formal assessment will be conducted at the end of the lesson to test students' knowledge on verbs, adjectives, and adverbs.

Academic Language – Language Function

Students will be asked to identify verbs, adjectives, and adverbs.

Academic Language – Language Vocabulary

The following are vocabulary words: verbs, adjectives, and adverbs.

Academic Language – Language Demand

The academic language demands the students will be using to participate in the tasks are writing and listening. Students will be asked to listen as I instruct the classroom. Students will be asked to write a sentence on the SMART Board. Students will be given a KWL worksheet to document information they know and what want to learn. During think-pair-share, the students will be given worksheet to document their thoughts.

Instructional Resources

None

Instructional Materials

The following are material used during the instruction:

- SMART Board

- KWL Chart (worksheets)

- Instructional Worksheets

- Posters

- Jeopardy game

Instructional Environment – Modifications/Adaptations

The instruction is planned to allow the students with various learning modes to participate. Modes include group/partner activities, independent work, visualize pictures/information, jeopardy game, and written assignments.

Students will start the lesson by setting on the carpet, but when completing the worksheets, the students will be instructed to go back to their desks. This change will allow the students who have difficulty sitting/focusing in one spot for long time to refocus.

Appropriate font will be used on SMART Board and worksheets to allow individuals with difficulty in reading/writing small print. This will support one student with 504 plan for visual processing along with visual learners.

Learning Experience Four

Topic/Title: Identifying Verbs, Adjectives, and Adverbs

Level: 3rd Grade Instruction

Central Focus

The central focus is for the students to understand, recognize, and use nouns, pronouns, verbs, adjectives, and adverbs when reading and writing.

Educational Standards

CCSS.ELA-Literacy.L.3.1 - Demonstrate command of the conventions of standard English grammar and usage when writing or speaking.

CCSS.ELA-Literacy.L.3.1.a - Explain the function of nouns, pronouns, verbs, adjectives, and adverbs in general and their functions in particular sentences.

CCSS.ELA-Literacy.RI.3.1 - Ask and answer questions to demonstrate understanding of a text, referring explicitly to the text as the basis for the answers.

CCSS.ELA-Literacy.W.3.3 - Write narratives to develop real or imagined experiences or events using effective technique, descriptive details, and clear event sequences.

Objective(s)

The following are objectives associated with this lesson:

- read third grade level reading articles and ask and answer questions related to the reading articles

- recognize and explain nouns, pronouns, verbs, adjectives, and adverbs

- write short essay using nouns, pronouns, verbs, adjectives, and adverbs

Instructional Procedures (step by step instructional procedures)

Note: Students are sitting at round table.

Step 1: I will welcome the students to the classroom. I will explain we will be reading a third grade reading text to identify verbs, adjectives, and adverbs along with answer comprehension questions. Moreover, I will explain the big picture/central focus along with how this lesson connects to the central focus.

Step 2: To engage the students and activate prior knowledge, I will have the students complete a think-pair-share activity by giving them a worksheet with to identify verbs, adjectives, and adverbs in sentences. I will select students to share the answers they obtained with their partner.

Step 3: I will give each student a copy of the reading article. I will explain to the students we will read together by taking turns. Once we finish reading one paragraph, we will stop to underline the verbs, adjectives, and adverbs, and verbally discuss the use of the verbs, adjectives, and adverbs. Students will be asked to complete this on their own copy. Once completed, I will ask students to inform me what they identified, and I will document it on the SMART Board. Before moving forward, I will make sure that all nouns, pronouns, verbs, adjectives, and adverbs have been identified.

Step 4: I will ask students comprehension questions regarding the paragraph. The students will be asked to provide the answer, but also explain how verbs, adjectives, and adverbs supported them in answering the questions.

Step 5: We will complete step three and four for each paragraph in the reading article.

Step 6: Students will be completing in-class essay. The students will be asked to write a response to a prompt, in which they will have to underline using nouns, pronouns, verbs, adjectives, and adverbs.

Closure Procedures

To close the lesson, I will recap all the lessons, and I call on students to explain to me the meaning of one of the words (nouns, pronouns, verbs, adjectives, and adverbs) introduced in the lessons.

Assessment(s)

I will be informally assessing the students when reading together (Step 4 and 5).

A formal assessment (writing essay) will be conducted at the end of the lesson to test students' knowledge on nouns, pronouns, verbs, adjectives, and adverbs.

Academic Language – Language Function

Students will be asked to identify noun, pronoun, verb, adjective, or adverb along with identify details of passage to answer comprehension questions.

Academic Language – Language Vocabulary

The following are vocabulary words: nouns, pronouns, verbs, adjectives, and adverbs

Academic Language – Language Demand

The academic language demands the students will be using to participate in the tasks are writing, reading, and listening. Students will be asked to listen to myself and other students while reading. The students will be asked to write a short essay in which they underline nouns, pronouns, verbs, adjectives, and adverbs.

Instructional Resources

None

Instructional Materials

The following are material used during the instruction:

- SMART Board

- KWL Chart (worksheets)

- Instructional Worksheets

- Reading Articles

Instructional Environment – Modifications/Adaptations

The instruction is planned to allow the students with various learning modes to participate. Modes include group/partner activities, independent work, visualize pictures/information, jeopardy game, and written assignments.

Appropriate font will be used on SMART Board and worksheets to allow individuals with difficulty in reading/writing small print. This supports one student with 504 plan for visual processing along with visual learners.

Students will start the lesson by setting on the carpet, but when completing the worksheets, the students will be instructed to go back to their desks. This change will allow the students who have difficulty sitting/focusing in one spot for long time to refocus.

Instructional Material – Lesson 1 (Think Pair Share Worksheet)

Name: Date:

Think – Pair – Share
Activity

Noun

Pronoun

Nouns

What are nouns?

- Parts of speech that can be used as the subject of a sentence

- Nouns name a person, place or thing

Example of nouns

snake (thing)   James (person)   house (place)

  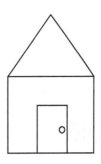

How to find nouns?

- Look for names, places, and things

- Names and places are sometimes capitalized

Practicing identifying nouns

- Kate and Juan were playing outside in the park until dark.

Pronouns

What are pronouns?

- Parts of speech that can be used as the subject of a sentence

- Pronoun is a word that is used in place of or stands for a noun

Example of common pronouns

I	You	He	She	It	We	Us	Me
	They	Its	Our	Your	Them		

What is antecedent?

The noun that the pronoun stands for is called the antecedent.

How to find pronouns?

- Remember common pronouns

- Connect the pronoun to the noun that is replaced

Practicing identifying pronouns

Jake bought the truck after he had collected the money.
NOTE: Noun is Jake and Pronoun is he.
Mark found his wallet, so he went to Marty and told her.
NOTE: Pronouns from left to right are: his, he, and her.
Did you identify the antecedent of his as Mark?
Did you identify the antecedent of he also as Mark?
Did you identify the antecedent of her as Marty?

noun

pronoun

noun

pronoun

noun

pronoun

Sentence: The butterfly was huge and it went into every room in the house before leaving.

Identify the noun (s) and pronoun(s)

Nouns: butterfly, house, room

Pronoun(s): it (describing the butterfly)

Sentence: The birds were in the sky, and it was night time.

Identify the noun (s) and pronoun(s)

Noun: sky, birds

Pronoun(s): it   (describing the sky)

Think-Pair-Share

What are nouns?

What are pronouns?

Underline the noun(s) in the following sentence:

Alejandro was looking for a job for several years, and his brother finally helped him get a job at the local library.

Underline the pronouns in the following sentence:

Mr. Barry was a middle school teacher turned truck driver. He was able to deliver fast because of his extensive knowledge in the surrounding areas.

Write a sentence using at least one noun and one pronoun. Identify the noun and pronoun.

Sentence:

Noun(s):

Pronoun(s):

Playing Soccer

Soccer is played throughout the world. In most places except for the United States, soccer is known as football. The basic concept to soccer is two teams playing with a round ball on a field, and each team attempts to put the ball in the other team's goal. A player called the goalie guards the team's goal. These players are the only ones who can touch the ball with their arms and hands.

The other players move the ball by kicking it. They can also head a ball in the air using their heads, and they can run with the ball by dribbling it by kicking the ball to themselves with short, quick taps. To ensure that all rules are being strictly followed, a referee can call a foul if a player breaks a rule. The referee can give the other team a penalty kick or free kick.

Basic soccer uses inexpensive equipment, making one of the easiest games to play around the world. Many individuals come together and play soccer on a nice stretch of grass. They can use jersey, shorts, socks, cleats, and shin guards. Casually, playing in the neighborhood, tennis shoes can be used instead of shin guards. Cleats assist in gripping the grass so players can run and turn faster. Protecting your ankles and legs are very important when spinning, turning, kicking, and changing directions, and the cleats provide that protection.

The Rain Forest Environment

Rain forest is a very warm and wet forest habitat. It has thousands of plants and animals. Rain forests are found around the world, including South America, West Africa, and Australia. Plants and animals live in different parts of the rainforest. They can be found in of the strata (layer) of the rain forests: emergent, canopy, understory, and forest floor.

Emergents are the giant trees that are a lot higher than the typical canopy height. The tops of the tallest trees make up the emergent layer. Various types of birds are typically found in this layer, including mascaw and love birds.

Canopy is the upper parts of the trees, and trees in this layer may be as high as 100 feet. It protects the ground from sun and light rain. The environment is full of life and includes insects, birds, mammals, and more.

The understory layer is dark and hot. It is a tangle of shrubs, young trees, palms, and vines. Plants that rapidly grow tend to have large leaves. Anacondas, large snakes, live in the understory.

The forest floor is very warm and humid as very little sun reaches the forest floor. Fallen leaves, dead plants, and animals will decay (rot) rapidly. Large animals commonly live in this layer; some animals include tapir or jaguar.

Name: Date:

Think – Pair – Share

Activity

Adverb

Adjective

Verbs

Verbs

What are verbs?

- Necessary for a sentence to be complete

- A verb is a word which describes the action in a sentence

Examples of verb

- Juan likes to run.

- I am looking to buy a house.

- My computer broke, so I need to buy a new computer.

How to find verb?

- Think of the verb as the "doing" word

- A sentence will always have a verb to be a complete sentence.

Practice identifying verbs

- Kate and Juan were playing outside in the park until dark.

- Today, John will sit outside and do work, because he needs the sunlight.

Adverbs

What are adverbs?

- A word that describes a verb

- An adverb tells us when, where, and how about verbs, adjectives and even other adverbs

Example of adverbs

- The baby carried loudly.

- The brother drove faster than his friend.

- Everyone waited quietly for the news report.

How to find adverbs?

- Look out for words ending in "ing" or "er" or "est"

- Find the verb and see if there is an adjective around the verb

Practice identifying adverbs

- Gabby, my oldest sister, drove slowly by her mother's house.

- In March, everyone was hearing about not having a class party because a student was extremely rude.

Adjectives

What are adjectives?

- An adjective is a word that tells us more about a noun or a pronoun.

- An adjective describes or modifies a noun.

Example of adjectives

large city – red rose – new house – small butterfly – bright, yellow sun

How to find adjectives?

- Adjectives usually answer three questions about the nouns they describe:

    What kind of? - How many? - Which one(s)?

Practice identifying adjectives

- The brothers walk their huge dog around the block.

- My group used purple markers to make our poster.

Sentence: The bright, yellow sun was going to cause hot temperatures.

Identify the adjective(s).

Adjective(s): bright, yellow

Sentence: The sky was very cloudy as rain was going to start soon.

Identify the verb (s).

Verb(s): start

Noun	Pronoun	Adjective	Verb	Adverb	Mix Review
100	100	100	100	100	100
200	200	200	200	200	200
300	300	300	300	300	300
400	400	400	400	400	400
500	500	500	500	500	500

Name: Date:

Verbs, Adverbs, and Adjectives

Question 1

Write a sentence that has both verb and adjective.

Question 2

Write a student that has verb, adverb, and adjective.

Playing Soccer

Soccer is played throughout the world. In most places except for the United States, soccer is known as football. The basic concept to soccer is two teams playing with a round ball on a field, and each team attempts to put the ball in the other team's goal. A player called the goalie guards the team's goal. These players are the only ones who can touch the ball with their arms and hands.

The other players move the ball by kicking it. They can also head a ball in the air using their heads, and they can run with the ball by dribbling it by kicking the ball to themselves with short, quick taps. To ensure that all rules are being strictly followed, a referee can call a foul if a player breaks a rule. The referee can give the other team a penalty kick or free kick.

Basic soccer uses inexpensive equipment, making one of the easiest games to play around the world. Many individuals come together and play soccer on a nice stretch of grass. They can use jersey, shorts, socks, cleats, and shin guards. Casually, playing in the neighborhood, tennis shoes can be used instead of shin guards. Cleats assist in gripping the grass so players can run and turn faster. Protecting your ankles and legs are very important when spinning, turning, kicking, and changing directions, and the cleats provide that protection.

Task 1: Part D – Literacy Assessments

Assessment: Lesson 1 – KWL Chart

K What do we already know?	W What do we want to know?	L What have we learned?

Assessment: Lesson 1 – Worksheet

Nouns and Pronouns

QUESTION 1

Underline the pronoun(s) in the sentence below.

The house is very big because it has five bedrooms and two game rooms.

QUESTION 2

Change the underline word/words to a pronoun.

Tyler played video games with <u>Miguel and Ramon</u>.

QUESTION 3

Underline the noun(s) in the sentence below.

The sky has been very cloudy in the last several days due to possible hurricane.

QUESTION 4

The underline pronoun describes what noun. Underline the answer.

Melissa is not happy with her grade on the last homework assignment, so <u>she</u> is going to talk her teacher, Ms. Fontenot.

QUESTION 5

Underline the pronoun(s) in the sentence below.

If I eat all of these fruits, father will let me play television.

QUESTION 6

Underline the noun(s) in the sentence below.

Andrea is very nice person, and she has a lot of friends at school.

Assignment: Lesson 2 – (Worksheet Writing Activity)

Name: Student:

Assignment: Write one paragraph about a sport you have played.

_____

_____

_____

_____

_____

_____

_____

_____

Verbs, Adverbs, and Adjectives

QUESTION 1

Underline the verb(s) in the sentence below.

Tyler played video games with Miguel and Ramon.

QUESTION 2

Add an adjective to the sentence below.

She wore a _____ sweater to the party.

QUESTION 3

Underline the adverb(s) in the sentence below.

The sky turned very cloudy in the last several days due to possible hurricane.

QUESTION 4

Explain the different between verb and adverb.

QUESTION 5

Underline the verb(s) and adjective (s) in the sentence below.

If I eat all of these red apples, father will let me play television.

QUESTION 6

Underline the adjective(s) in the sentence below.

Mike is very rude person, and he gets in trouble every day; he is going to have to go to the principal's office.

Personal Essay Assignment

Select one prompt to write a short essay

Prompt 1: Write a 2-3 paragraph essay about a school field trip you have gone on in the past.

Prompt 2: Write a 2-3 paragraph essay about a school field trip you want to go in the future.

Requirements:

- Use nouns, pronouns, verbs, adverbs, and adjectives

- Select one paragraph and underline in blue ink pen all nouns and pronouns

- Select one paragraph and underline in black ink pen all verbs, adverbs, and adjectives

Name: **Date:**

Instruction: Select one prompt to write your short essay

Prompt 1: Write a 2-3 paragraph essay about a school field trip you have gone on in the past.

Prompt 2: Write a 2-3 paragraph essay about a school field trip you want to go in the future.

_____

_____

_____

_____

_____

_____

_____

_____

Task 1 Part E: Planning Commentary

QUESTION 1 – Central Focus

Part A

The central focus is for the students to understand, recognize, and use nouns, pronouns, verbs, adjectives, and adverbs. Recognizing parts of speech (nouns, pronouns, verbs, adverbs, and adjectives) by identifying/underlining is the essential literacy strategy that will support students in strengthening writing with appropriate use of parts of speech. Identifying via underlining is appropriate essential literacy strategy when getting early grade level students to recognize parts of speech. Related skill necessary to achieve the central focus and essential literacy strategy is writing convention. Proper writing convention is important to have for clear and concise essay.

Part B

Lesson 1

In lesson 1,

In lesson 1, the standard is associated with explaining the function of nouns and pronouns. The objectives include understanding, identifying, and writing related to nouns and pronouns. The students learn about nouns and pronouns via direct instruction. Afterwards, students complete an in-class activity in which they are required to write a sentence on the whiteboard underlining nouns/pronouns. Moreover, the students are required to complete a worksheet in which they have to underline the nouns/pronouns. In order to write sentences and obtain full credit, the students must follow proper writing convention.

Lesson 2

In lesson 2, a reading and writing connection exist as students are required to identify nouns and pronouns in a reading article. They are also required to explain the use of the nouns and pronouns. In this lesson one, students will be completing an activity in pairs involving writing one paragraph about a sport they have played. The students will then switch the papers with their partner. After switching, the students will underline the nouns and pronouns. Then, the papers will be given back to the original writer, and the students will be asked to grade the work of their partner. To complete this activity, the students will be applying the related skill of writing convection. After writing using proper convention, the students will be able to apply the essential literacy strategy.

Lesson 3

In lesson 3, the standard is associated with explaining the function of verbs, adverbs, and adjectives. The objectives include understanding, identifying, and writing related to verbs, adverbs, and adjectives. The students learn about verbs, adverbs, and adjectives via direct instruction. Afterwards, students participate in a jeopardy game requiring them to identify verbs, adverbs, and adjectives; some of the questions involve students underlining the nouns/pronouns. Moreover, the students are required to complete a worksheet in which they have underline verbs, adverbs, and adjectives. In order to write sentences and obtain full credit, the students must follow proper writing convention.

142

Lesson 4

In lesson 4, the objectives require the students to read a passage and to underline verbs, adverbs, and adjectives. Students will be asked comprehension questions for which they can use verbs, adverbs, and adjectives to support them in answering the questions. The objectives also involve writing a short essay. They will write on a prompt, and they will have to underline the nouns, pronouns, verbs, adverbs, and adjectives. Underling nouns, pronouns, verbs, adverbs, and adjectives, allow the students to see ways to use these parts of speech. In addition, these approaches will strength students' ability to use the parts of speech appropriately in the composition. Students will not be able to underline until they write, which require the related skill of proper writing convection.

Part C

In lesson 1, the students will be introduced to nouns and pronouns, and they will complete various activities (participating in think-pair-share, writing sentences on SMART Board, and completing worksheets). In doing these activities, the students will be required to underline the nouns and pronouns, and apply related skill of proper writing convection. In lesson 2, the students read an article in which they will have to underline nouns and pronouns. In addition, the lesson will require students to participate in a paired activity in which they will write paragraph and underline nouns/pronouns giving opportunity to connect essential literacy strategy and related skill. In lesson three, the students will be introduced to verbs, adverbs, and adjectives, and they will be completing various activities (think-pair-share and jeopardy game). The jeopardy game will also include questions regarding nouns and pronouns, connecting to prior learning. Lesson 4 builds on the previous lessons as students will be required to underline verbs, adverbs, and adjectives in the reading article. In addition, students will be required to write an essay in which they have to underline nouns, pronouns, verbs, adverbs, and adjectives. All lessons are connected as knowledge from previous lessons is incorporated in subsequent lessons. The related skill of writing convection is connected to the essential literacy strategy as the students are required to underline in most of the writing activities.

QUESTION 2 – Knowledge of Students to Inform Teaching

Part A

The central focus requires the students to gain understanding, recognizing, and using parts of speech (nouns, pronouns, verbs, adverbs, and adjectives). In order to participate in the learning activities, the students need to know how to read and write. The students know how to read at a third grade level and know how to compose sentences. Students have gained reading comprehension at the third grade level and continue to strength the ability to read/comprehend at the third grade level. The students are aware of the concept of recalling and they can recall details and facts, but they still are continuing to be more proficient with recalling. The students have written sentences and likely unknowingly used nouns, pronouns, verbs, adverbs, and adjectives. The students have basic understanding of writing convection (spelling, capitalization, punctuation, and grammar). The students also are aware of the concept of writing, and they can write complete sentences in addition to 1-2 paragraphs. The two English learners do struggle with writing and have minimal mistakes, but they do understand what constitutes a complete sentence. The student with mild speech disorder/struggling reader is the one student who had a long journey to achieve reading/comprehending at the third grade level, so this student will need repetition and more time to process information.

Part B

My students reside in a suburban area with much diversity in cultural and ethnicity. In my learning segment, I have five students of different ethnicities/races: two Hispanic students, one Pakistani student, one Asian student, one African American student, and one Caucasian American. The Asian student communicates a lot about her family and events she attends within her family. She celebrates culture holidays and goes back to her home country during the summer. In addition, the Hispanic student has talked about his travels to Mexico. These students all attend school from 8 AM to 4 PM and attend after school activities. Monday and Wednesday they receive additional academic support afterschool, and Tuesday and Thursday the students engage in physical/sport/outside activities. During the weekends, the students spend time with family or engage in outdoor activities; some of the students are involved in community sports activities. Four of the students I am instructing are bilingual, but only two of those are identified as English learners. The students are all at the appropriate level for reading, but no student has been identified as gifted/talented in reading, writing, or language skills.

One of my students has undergone eye surgery few years ago. The student takes special eye drops as a part of his treatment. Moreover, the student has difficulty with small print. This student learning difficulty is taken into consideration during lesson planning development.

Last year, most of these students went to the zoo, and they have talked about the experience. Also, the students have talk a lot about what they do outdoors. The students are interested in being outside. Including reading articles related to the outside environments engages the students in participating.

I have noticed that the students are very attached to technology. Most of them talk about games they play on Ipads and other tablets. In fact, when they use the SMART Board, none of the students have difficulty. In fact, they compete to have opportunity using the SMART Board, showing me that they have previous experience in using the SMART Board.

QUESTION 3 – Supporting Students' Literacy Learning

In developing the lesson plans and activities, I took into account the constructivist theory, which states that individuals work best when actively building on current and past knowledge. Students have gained reading comprehension knowledge and writing skills in previous grade. They might have unknowingly used nouns, pronouns, verbs, adverbs, and adjectives without paying close attention to the details and the functions. Students know how to write, and with learning about the parts of speech, students can strength writing abilities.

Differentiation was another aspect taken into account when planning these learning experiences. According to Carol Tomlinson, students have various learning readiness levels, and Tomlinson encourages differentiation to personalize learning to fit individuals' need to increase learning opportunities. The student with mild speech disorder (also struggling reader) requires repetitions to allow him to maintain knowledge. Repetition also supports my English learners. In my learning experiences, I start by teaching nouns and pronouns, and I revisit them in the remaining lessons. Having exposure to the concept multiple times will increase the ability to maintain knowledge.

My students also like to communicate with one another, so including think-pair-share activities gives a different opportunity to engage in learning. Two of my students have to write down information to remember what they learned, and using the KWL chart is a good tool to support their learning needs. One of my students has difficulty with sight and two students are visual learners, so I make sure the print is large enough to support to learning.

Knowing that I had English learners, a struggling reader, and no gifted/talented reading/writing students, I constructed my lessons to ensure activities were grade appropriate. I also made sure to take into account students' interest. Most students like to be outside and expressed enjoyment during the zoo field trip, so I included reading article that were related to animals and the outside environment. My students like to play sports, so I included a reading article on soccer. Knowing the students like to use the SMART Board, I incorporated that into my instruction. Having knowledge of the personal assets of the students, I was able to incorporate different learning modes that were helpful for each student. This approach applies Howard Gardner's Theory of Multiple Intelligence, which focuses on how potential is connected to individual's learning performances and individual's distinctive skills (called "intelligences"). According to Gardner, planning lessons on each student's "intelligences" helps in learning and gaining stronger understanding

Part B

My planned supports and instructional strategies are beneficial to all students, including English learners and special education students.

One instructional strategy used will be repetition. The student with mild speech disorder (also struggling reader) requires repetition to allow him to maintain knowledge. Repetition also supports my English learners. Repetition is not limited to just supporting students with needs, but all students in maintaining knowledge. In my learning experiences, I will introduce nouns and pronouns in the first lesson, but made sure to revisit them in the remaining lessons. In addition, I will introduce verbs, adverbs, and adjectives in the third lesson, but will have activities to further develop the students' knowledge in the fourth lesson.

In my learning experiences, I will use a number of planned supports: KWL chart, posters with pictures, SMART Board, and large print reading articles and worksheets. Filling out the KWL chart will support all students as they are able to write what they know, what they want to learn, and what they learned. Reflecting back on the KWL chart will allow them to see the progression in learning and provide confidence. Confidence is essential in learning, especially at this age. The large print reading passages and worksheets are mainly for the individuals that have sight difficulties, but do support visual students as well. Using posters with pictures was a way to support visual students and support them in maintaining knowledge as visual supports have been linked to increasing retention of knowledge. In lesson three, I used a jeopardy game to engage all students. All the students like to play games and like to compete with one another. This was a good approach to actively engage all learners.

In lesson two and three, I will ask the students comprehension questions that required them to look for nouns, pronouns, verbs, adverbs, and adjectives to support them in answering questions. This approach will support all students in ensuring they understand the passages. Most importantly, this instructional strategy of stopping and discussing the reading article will support the struggling reader.

All the instructional approaches and planned supports align with Gardner's Theory of Multiple Intelligences, which focuses on how potential is connected to individual's learning performances and individual's distinctive skills (called "intelligences"). Tailoring lessons to give the students opportunity to use strong areas will contribute in students' achievement.

Part C

The following are common developmental approximations or common misconceptions related to the central focus:

- Some students may be confused that there are few common pronouns (he, she, it, they, them, etc), so they can memorize the pronouns and be successful at identifying pronouns. This is not correct. The best way to address this is by teaching the function of pronouns and how to identify them.

- Pronouns, adverbs, and adjectives need to be placed in the right position in sentence to ensure that it is properly describing the noun or verb. To support students in not making the mistake, students will be explained the importance of proper placement of pronouns, adverbs, and adjectives.

- One of the articles is related to a science subject area. Some students might not have the science background to be exposed to these science related articles. However, these learning experiences do not require science related knowledge. To address this developmental approximation, students will be encouraged to inform me if they do not understand a word in the passage.

QUESTION 4 – Supporting Literacy Development Through Language

Part A

Writing sentences/paragraphs is the language function.

Part B

In lesson four, the students are required to write an essay on a prompt. The directions require the students to use nouns, pronouns, verbs, adverbs, and adjectives. The students also are required to underline the nouns, pronouns, verbs, adverbs, and adjectives. By giving the students opportunity to write, the students are able to use language function (writing) to practice the essential literacy strategy (underlining).

Part C

Vocabulary: Students need to have understanding of nouns, pronouns, verbs, adverbs, and adjectives to able to write appropriately. Students will also have to read mentally what they write to be able to underline the nouns, pronouns, verbs, adverbs, and adjectives.

Syntax: Students need to properly arrange words and phrases to create well-formed sentences in a language.

Part D

The following instructional supports were included in the lesson to help students understand, develop, and use identified language demands:

- Worksheet – After having the student learn and practice, the students will be asked to complete a worksheet associated with the objective(s) of the lesson.

- Posters – Posters are developed to show students the concepts introduced with example sentences.

- Reading Articles – Including reading articles and having the students underline the nouns, pronouns, verbs, adverbs, and adjectives allows students to practice but also see how nouns, pronouns, verbs, adverbs, and adjectives are used in sentences. In lesson two and three, I used the same reading article only to allow my struggling reader and English learners to easily understand the passage and focus on finding verbs, adverbs, and adjectives.

- KWL Chart – The KWL chart (included in instructional material) will allow the students to document information they will learn in the learning experiences. Students will write the words associated with the science field in the learned column.

- Jeopardy Game – Students will play a jeopardy game to apply the knowledge acquired for nouns, pronouns, verbs, adverbs, and adjectives. Giving students opportunity to apply knowledge will support them in using nouns, pronouns, verbs, adverbs, and adjectives appropriately in writing.

QUESTION 5 – Monitoring Student Learning

Part A

Lesson 1

In lesson one, informally, I will observe the students when writing their sentences on the SMART Board. Students will be asked to underline the nouns/pronouns, allowing me to see students use of literacy strategy. In addition, the students are required to complete a worksheet that requires them to show evidence of learning associated with the objective(s) of the lesson. The worksheet gives students the opportunity to underline nouns/pronouns.

Lesson 2

I will be informally assessing the students when reading together to identify nouns and pronouns. Students will be required to work in pairs to write paragraphs in which they will be required to underline nouns and pronouns, allowing me to see students use of literacy strategy in composing text. In addition, the students will complete a worksheet to test student's knowledge on nouns and pronouns.

Lesson 3

In lesson three, I will be informally assessing the students during the jeopardy game. The game will be designed to give students opportunity to compose text and use essential literacy strategy. The students scores obtain during the game will also allow me to see best performance in the classroom and those who need additional support. In addition, the students will complete a worksheet to test student's knowledge on verbs, adverbs, and adjectives.

Lesson 4

I will be informally assessing the students when reading together to identify verbs, adverbs, and adjectives. Students will be asked to write a short essay, which I will grade using a rubric.

Part B

The assessments planned give fair opportunities for all students with specific needs. During the reading in lesson two and four, the students take turn reading and answering comprehension questions. This supports all students in understanding the content, but especially, the student with mild speech disorder (who is also a struggling reader) as he will read the article in lesson four.

The worksheets, reading articles, and posters were all of large print documents to support my student with visual processing disorder. The worksheets will have large font to ensure the student does not have difficulty processing the words visually.

The assessments appeal to various different needs by applying Gardener's theory of multiple intelligences. Students will practice with the material by worksheets, paired activities, group activities, and jeopardy game to apply to students' development of knowledge on the unit. The purpose of using different intelligences allows the students to make a deeper connection with the material.

English learners are taken into account for the assessments as guided reading will be completed during the lesson. The pictures in the reading article give visual cues. In addition, the English learners students need guided notes to support them in writing. The underline strategy supports these learners as they will have review their writing, allowing them to find mistakes.

Task 2 Part A: Video Recording

The video summary is provided below for the Elementary Education – Literacy assessment portfolio.

- Instruction was done with six students as outlined in the context of learning
- Instruction took place in a classroom.
- There are 10 desks in the classroom with a teacher desk. Also, there are several circle tables along with a carpet area.
- Clip 1 included lesson 1 from Step 4 to Step 9 (refer to instructional procedures section of the lesion plan).
- Clip 2 included lesson 3 from Step 2 to Step 4 (refer to instructional procedures section of the lesson plan).

The remaining page is intentionally left blank.

Task 2 Part B: Instruction Commentary

QUESTION 1

Clip 1 shows lesson plan 1 while Clip 2 shows lesson plan 3.

QUESTION 2 – Promoting a Positive Learning Environment

Part A

Giving direct eye contact, listening to my students, and focusing on my students are ways I demonstrated mutual respect and responsiveness. As the students read the article in lesson 2, I made sure to listen carefully, but I also made sure others were listening. For example, when one student was looking around the class while another student was reading, I gave hand gestures to the student to pay attention (Clip 2, timestamp: 3:30). When having the students respond to check for understanding questions during reading, I notice one student was not responding, so I engaged him in the conversation (Clip 2 timestamp: 4:01).

One way I showed rapport with my students is giving all students opportunity to respond and participate. For example, I made sure that I had six index (one for each student) to pick to write a sentence on the SMART Board (Clip1, timestamp: 10:32). As I planned my lessons, I made sure to include opportunities to call on all of the students to answer questions, ask questions, and read aloud. For example, I made sure that three students read aloud in lesson 2 (Clip 2, timestamp: 7:32) and the other three read aloud in lesson 4. I made sure not to call on the same student twice in a row to allow everyone equal opportunity to respond.

Delivering positive feedback and asking comprehension questions were another way to show respect and challenge the students to continue with the learning. When the students answered questions correctly, I made sure to give positive comments. Giving the students positive comments allowed them to continue with the learning activities. For example, when the student answered the question "What is the noun in the last sentence of the paragraph?" correctly, I said, "This is an excellent response. Good Job." (Clip 2, timestamp: 6:32). If the students provided wrong answers to questions, I did not directly give them the correct answer. I directed them to look at the passage and ask questions to guide the student in the right direction, which challenged the student to look deeper (Clip 2, timestamp: 4:32).

QUESTION 3 – Engaging Students in Learning

Part A

Throughout all the lessons, multiple opportunities existed to engage the students in developing the essential literacy strategy and the related skill. The essential literacy strategy was underline parts of speech (nouns, pronouns, verbs, adverbs, and adjectives). While instructing the students, I showed them a sentence and underlined the noun/pronoun (Clip 1, timestamp: 2:32). In lesson 1, I had the students write a sentence on the whiteboard and underline the pronoun or noun (Clip 1, timestamp: 12:32). To construct the sentences, the students had to use proper writing convection.

150

In lesson 2, the students were again engaged in the essential literacy skill during the think-pair-share activity and reading activity. For the think-pair-share activity, the students were required to underline nouns/pronouns on pre-written sentences and student written sentences. The students also were involving in underlining nouns and pronouns while reading the article.

Part B

The topic of the articles used are related to students' personal interest as most of these students went to the zoo and talked about how they liked the trip. All students are involved in sports in school and communities, so getting them exposed to knowledge on a common sport related to students' interest.

Throughout lesson one, I use the SMART Board to instruct, but I also have the students come up to the SMART Board and write sentences (Clip 1, timestamp 11:02 – 12:32). I have noticed that the students are very attached to technology. Most of them talk about the games they play on Ipads and other tablets. In fact, when they use the SMART Board, none of the students have difficulty.

The students know how to read at a third grade level and continue to develop on reading comprehension. Students have all gained reading comprehension at the third grade level and are in process of continuing to strengthen reading and comprehension at the third grade level. This lesson is linked to prior knowledge of reading. The students also have written sentences and 1-2 paragraphs in previous classes. The students have basic knowledge of sentence, but not have gone into detail lessons on nouns, pronouns, verbs, adverbs, or adjectives. These learning experiences connect to prior knowledge of the students, but expand students' knowledge to become better writers. Students know the concept of underlining, but they have not used underlining to identify parts of speech in the past. At this age in learning, the literacy strategy supports the students on accomplishing the objectives of the lesson, learning to constantly recognize parts of speech, and achieving the central focus.

QUESTION 4 – Deepening Student Learning During Instruction

Part A

To elicit and build on student responses, I engaged students in instruction by asking checking for understanding. For example, when I was teaching about nouns, I asked the students to identify the nouns in the example problem (Clip 1, timestamp: 6:43). The questions encouraged students to review the information that was previously presented. I also elicit responses by using posters. I knew my students like images and posters, so including those tools grabbed students' attention. When I presented the first poster in lesson one, all the students responded (Clip 1, timestamp: 7:52) When I received weak responses, I challenged the student to look carefully and encourage another attempt. For example, when I presented the second poster in lesson one, the students' identified the noun, but I got no response when asked about the pronoun. I asked the students to read and to look carefully, and two students were able to state the pronoun (Clip 1, timestamp: 8:03). The challenging and pushing the student had a positive impact to learning.

The structure of the lesson allowed me to build on students' responses and elicit responses. Having well organized lessons that built on student knowledge prevents the students from struggling, allowing them to provide responses to questions. In lesson one, I had the students learn about pronouns and nouns only; I did not introduce verbs, adverbs or adjectives because I knew these students included struggling readers and English learners (Clip 1, timestamp: 3:43 – 10:03). I did not want to overwhelm the students and discourage my students. Taking this approach, allowed the students to process the information and participate in learning activities. In lesson two, I did an activity for students to further practice and apply the knowledge developed in lesson one. In lesson three, I introduce verbs, adverbs, and adjectives, and I used a jeopardy game to elicit students' participation. Lesson four involved student using the information presented in previous lessons to read article and underline verbs, adverbs, and adjectives. Also, in lesson four, the students were required to write a short essay on a writing prompt and underline nouns, pronouns, verbs, adverbs, and adjectives.

To promote the application of learning, I provide positive feedback throughout the lessons. For example, when the student answered the question "What are the noun in the last sentence of the paragraph?" correctly, I said, "This is an excellent response. Good Job." (Clip 2, timestamp: 6:32). Positive feedback keeps the students engaged to continue the learning process. When the students provided incorrect response, I gave positive feedback and used tools, to elicit correct response. For example, I asked the students "What is the noun in the sentence: Basic soccer uses inexpensive equipment, making this an easy game to play." The student was incorrect. I said, "Good try", but I asked the student to look carefully and try again. (Clip 2, timestamp: 3:55). Giving the student the positive feedback and encouraging him to look at the reading article, the student was able to provide correct response.

Part B

The following are shown in the video that demonstrate modeling of essential literacy strategy and supporting the students in practicing/applying strategy:

- I used direct instruction modeling to explain the concept of nouns and pronouns. I showed example problems on underlining pronouns and nouns (Clip 1, timestamp: 4:30).

- I used posters to allow students to practice using the information on nouns and pronouns (Clip 1, timestamp: 5:04).

- Before having the students write their sentence on the whiteboard, I wrote an example sentence and underlined the noun and pronoun (Clip 1, timestamp: 5:43).

- In lesson two, I started the reading of the article to capture student's attention. Moreover, I also explained to the students that "soccer" is the noun in the first sentence.

- In lesson two, I gave students the opportunity to practice essential literacy strategy by stopping and having them underline nouns and pronouns (Clip 2, timestamp: 4:21).

QUESTION 5 – Analyzing Teaching

Part A

The following are changes I recommend to better support the students:

- I have several students who are visual students, so I could have included more instructional material that targeted visual students, such as a video. Having a video targeting third grade interest can be powerful in learning.

- I had individual students fill out KWL chart, but a better addition is to have a class KWL where I write what individual students wrote on their chart.

- When asking the student with speech disorder to identify noun, I could have given him more wait time to respond before providing guidance (Clip 2, timestamp: 4:23).

Part B

The following are reasons for why the changes recommended will improve student learning:

- Having instructional material targeting students need, such as video, engage the students more and allow exploration of knowledge in more concrete manner, which supported by Piaget's stages of cognitive development. With third graders typically in the concrete operational stage having concept connected to concrete situation supports learning.

- Having a large KWL chart and updating it throughout the learning, engages the student. In addition, having a large KWL chart will be a reminder of what the students' know and what they want to know. Most importantly, the large KWL will support my student who has a visual processing disorder and visual learners.

- Giving additional time is supported by Mary Budd Rowe, an educational researcher. Giving the students longer response time helps the students verbalize the response. Teachers are able to use the response to have a better and in-depth discussion.

- To prevent students from struggling during the writing assignment in lesson four, I included two prompts (students to select prompt) that were general that all students can write without difficulty. By not struggling to write, the students are encouraged to complete activity of underlining nouns, pronouns, verbs, adverbs, and adjectives.

Name: ▮▮▮▮   **Date:** ▮▮▮▮▮

Instruction: Select **one** prompt to write your short essay.

Prompt 1: Write a 2-3 paragraph essay about a past school field trip you have gone on.

Prompt 2: Write a 2-3 paragraph essay about a school field trip you want to go in the future.

Last year, my class went to the zoo
and it was the best trip. The trip
started in the morning. All the students
went on big yellow bus to the zoo. Rigth
when we arrived at the zoo the staff was
nice. They gave us safety stuff and rules.
The staff promply divided students into
3 groups and we all had a person in
charge.

I really like the area of the birds. The zoo had many different kinds of wonderful looking birds. Some of the birds loudly talked. I was suprised becaused I did not knew that zoos kept birds that talked. I took a lot of pictures in the bird section because it was my favorte area. Another wonderful feature was the many blue and red fishes. In this area I took a lot of pictures with my friends.

The best part of the trip was

eating lunch at the restraunt located
in the zoo. The teacher suprised all
of the studentswhen suprised she to
us about eating at restraunt. I was
really happy about eating at the
restraunt. I got tacos and fries.

I truly enjoyed going to the zoo and
enjoyed the day. I told my teacher we
should do this more often.

Name: ▓▓▓▓▓▓   **Date:** ▓▓▓▓▓▓

Instruction: Select one prompt to write your short essay

Prompt 1: Write a 2-3 paragraph essay about a school field trip you have gone on in the past.

Prompt 2: Write a 2-3 paragraph essay about a school field trip you want to go in the future.

For a field trip I like to go to an amusement park. Back in Texas I went to a lot of amusement parks with my family, and I really liked it and had fun. My brother and I went on many fun rides all day. We go early in the morning and leave night time, Since I move to Florida I have not gone to any amusement parks. I like to see what amusement parks offer here.

I want the field trip to include doing tour of park and riding all the rides. I want to go on the dark rides and water rides. Students work hard everyday and I think having a fun day at the amusement park with classmate is a good idea. Students need to have a fun day with classmates outside of school.

Name: **Date:**

Instruction: Select **one** prompt to write your short essay.

Prompt 1: Write a 2-3 paragraph essay about a past school field trip you have gone on.

Prompt 2: Write a 2-3 paragraph essay about a school field trip you want to go in the future.

In first grade, my class went on field trip to the park. When we get to the park, teacher had us set on the green grass, and she gave Worksheet package. Each worksheet had a picture and explain what it was. Teacher explained to us what the picture was and pointed it out to us. I liked this lesson because it was different.

When the lesson was done the
teacher let us take resess time in park.
We played ball and ran and tag. I
enormously liked the big park. There
is a lot to do. When we were done
playing, the teacher had box lunch
for us to eat at the park. At the end
teacher told us what we learned
and why we did lesson at the park.
Then we went back to classroom.

Task 3: Part B – Evidence of Feedback

Focus Learner 1 – Feedback

Focus Student 1

Total Score: (19)/20

Name: ███████

Date of Evaluation: 12/3/15

Evaluation Criteria

	Needs Improvement	Acceptable	Good	Outstanding
Content The student provides an organized, meaningful response to one of the prompts.	1	2	3	④
Nouns/Pronouns The student properly uses and underlines nouns/pronouns.	1	2	3	④
Verbs/Adverbs The student properly uses and underlines verbs/adverbs.	1	2	3	④
Adjectives The student properly uses and underlines adjectives.	1	2	3	④
Related Skill (Writing Conventions) The student writes complete sentences by following writing convections. The student writes with accurate use of punctuation and capitalization rules along with spelling correctly.	1	2	③	4

Scoring: (Outstanding (17-20)) Proficient (14-16) Learning (11-13) Below Average (0-10)

Comments: You provided good details. You also did a good job with underlining verbs, adverbs, adjectives, nouns and pronouns. Watch out for spelling!!!   Great Job!!!

161

Focus Student 1   Score: 19/20

Name: ███   **Date:** ███

Instruction: Select **one** prompt to write your short essay.

Prompt 1: Write a 2-3 paragraph essay about a past school field trip you have gone on.

Prompt 2: Write a 2-3 paragraph essay about a school field trip you want to go in the future.

Last year, my class went to the zoo,
and it was the best trip. The trip
started in the morning. All the students
went on a big yellow bus to the zoo. Right
when we arrived at the zoo the staff was
nice. They gave us safety stuff and rules.
The staff promply divided students into
3 groups, and we all had a person in
charge.

Good job! Excellent!!

Focus Student 1

I really liked the area of the
birds. The zoo had many different
Kinds of wonderful looking birds. Some
of the birds loudly talked. I was suprised
because I did not ~~knew~~ know that zoos
kept birds that talked. I took a lot of
pictures in the bird section because
it was my favorite area. Another
wonderful feature was the many
blue and red fishes. In this area I
took a lot of pictures with my friends.
    The best part of the trip was

163

Focus Student 1

                                                    restaurant
eating lunch at the ~~restraunt~~ located

in the zoo. The teacher suprised all

of the studentswhen ~~suprised~~ she told
                                  the
us about eating at restraunt. I was

really happy about eating at the

restraunt. I got tacos and fries.

   I truly enjoyed going to the zoo and

enjoyed the day. I told my teacher we

should do this more often.
                              Did you review this
                                            page?

164

Focus Learner 2 – Feedback

Focus Student 2

Name: _____

Total Score: (11)/20

Date of Evaluation: 12/3/15

Evaluation Criteria

	Needs Improvement	Acceptable	Good	Outstanding
Content *The student provides an organized, meaningful response to one of the prompts.*	(1)	2	3	4
Nouns/Pronouns *The student properly uses and underlines nouns/pronouns.*	1	(2)	3	4
Verbs/Adverbs *The student properly uses and underlines verbs/adverbs.*	1	(2)	3	4
Adjectives *The student properly uses and underlines adjectives.*	1	2	(3)	4
Related Skill (Writing Conventions) *The student writes complete sentences by following writing convections. The student writes with accurate use of punctuation and capitalization rules along with spelling correctly.*	1	2	(3)	4

Scoring: Outstanding (17-20) Proficient (14-16) (Learning (11-13)) Below Average (0-10)

Comments: Very good with underlining pronouns, but there is work to be done with nouns. Underlining verbs is another area to work on. Also, to increase "content" score more details are needed. Good job with adjectives and adverbs. Also, we need to practice on using commas.

Name: **Date:**

Instruction: Select one prompt to write your short essay

Prompt 1: Write a 2-3 paragraph essay about a school field trip you have gone on in the past.

Prompt 2: Write a 2-3 paragraph essay about a school field trip you want to go in the future.

For a field trip, I like to go to an amusement park. Back in Texas, I (verb) went to a lot of amusement parks with my family, and I really liked it and (verb) had fun. My brother and I (verb) went on many (adjective) fun rides all day. We go early in the morning and leave night time. Since I move to Florida, I have not (verb) gone to any amusement parks. I like to

Focus Student 2

(verb SEE) What amusement parks (verb offer) here.

I want the (noun field trip) to include

doing a tour it the park and riding all the

rides. I want to go on the dark rides

and water rides. Students work hard

every day, and I think having a

fun (noun day) at the amusement park with

classmate is a good idea. Students

need to have a fun (noun day) with

classmates outside of (noun school).

Good job with pronouns!!!

Remember COMMAS are IMPORTANT

167

Focus Student 3

Name: ▓▓▓▓▓▓

Total Score: (15)/20

Date of Evaluation: 12/3/15

Evaluation Criteria

	Needs Improvement	Acceptable	Good	Outstanding
Content *The student provides an organized, meaningful response to one of the prompts.*	1	2	(3)	4
Nouns/Pronouns *The student properly uses and underlines nouns/pronouns.*	1	(2)	3	4
Verbs/Adverbs *The student properly uses and underlines verbs/adverbs.*	1	2	(3)	4
Adjectives *The student properly uses and underlines adjectives.*	1	2	3	(4)
Related Skill (Writing Conventions) *The student writes complete sentences by following writing convections. The student writes with accurate use of punctuation and capitalization rules along with spelling correctly.*	1	2	(3)	4

Scoring: <u>Outstanding (17-20)</u> (<u>Proficient (14-16)</u>) <u>Learning (11-13)</u> <u>Below Average (0-10)</u>

Comments: You included details, which is great. You also did very good with underlining pronouns, but we need to work on nouns. All in all, this was very good work and let us continue this way.

168

Focus Student 3   Score: 15/20

Name: **Date:**

Instruction: Select **one** prompt to write your short essay.

Prompt 1: Write a 2-3 paragraph essay about a past school field trip you have gone on.

Prompt 2: Write a 2-3 paragraph essay about a school field trip you want to go in the future.

In first grade, my class went on a
field trip to the (noun Park) When we got
to the park, the teacher had us set on
the green (noun grass) and she gave a Worksheet.
(noun Package). Each (noun worksheet) had a (noun picture)
and explained what it was. Teacher
explained to us what the picture was
and pointed it out to us. I liked
this lesson because it was different.

Good job with
Pronouns!!!

169

Focus Student 3

When the lesson was done, the
teacher let us take ~~recess~~ recess time in the park.
We played ball, and ran, and tag. I
enormously (verb liked) the big park. There
is a lot to do. When we were done
playing, the teacher had box lunches
for us to eat at the park. At the end,
the teacher told us what we learned
and why we did the lesson at the park.
Then we went back to classroom.

Almost had all of them
Underlined !!!

"the" is very common
to forget to write. Always read slowly to see if you
missed any "the"

170

Task 3: Part C – Literacy Assessment Commentary

QUESTION 1 – Analyzing Student Learning

Part A

The following are the objectives measured by the assessment selected:

- CCSS.ELA-Literacy.L.3.1 - Demonstrate command of the conventions of standard English grammar and usage when writing or speaking.

- CCSS.ELA-Literacy.L.3.1.a - Explain the function of nouns, pronouns, verbs, adjectives, and adverbs in general and their functions in particular sentences.

- CCSS.ELA-Literacy.W.3.3 - Write narratives to develop real or imagined experiences or events using effective technique, descriptive details, and clear event sequences.

Part B

Below is a table that shows learning for all students related to the criteria outlined in the evaluation criteria.

	Content	Nouns/Pronouns	Verbs/Adverbs	Adjectives	Writing Conventions	**Total**
Student 1	4	4	4	4	3	19
Student 2	1	2	2	3	3	11
Student 3	3	2	3	4	3	15
Student 4	3	3	3	3	3	15
Student 5	3	2	3	4	3	15
Student 6	4	3	4	4	3	18
Average	2.83	2.67	3.17	3.67	3.00	15.33

Part C

The scores for nouns and pronouns were the lowest, and this is because the students struggled with underlining the nouns. As seen in the sample works of the three students, they were all able to underline pronouns with no issues. The pronouns that the students used were basic and very common, so that is likely the reason for seeing this pattern. The nouns gave these students difficulty along with the other students. The entire class performed well with underlining adjectives as the average was the highest. All students obtain the same score in the related skills criteria. No student received outstanding marks on writing conventions because there were few errors in each of the students' response. At the same time, there were not many errors that would result in them receiving less than "Good". By not receiving "1" in any of the categories involving underlining (nouns/pronouns, verbs/adverbs, and adjectives), the students showed achievement in the essential literacy strategy, related skills, and central focus.

Also, no student received total score of below average. Student 2, individual with speech disorder, was close to receiving a below average score. This student needs constant practice to eventually obtain higher score. This student had a long journey to reach reading and writing comprehension at the third grade level. The two English learners (Student 4 and Student 5) received the same total score. Interesting, the student with visual processing disorder (Student 3) performed exactly the same as Student 5. The two students who do not have IEP or learning needs scored the highest (Student 1 and Student 6). In fact, both of those students received four in the content category. Students did forget to underline parts of speech, but no student improperly underlined parts of speech.

Part D

Not applicable.

QUESTION 2 – Feedback to Guide Further Learning

Part A

Feedback for the focus student was written directly on work sample and separate rubric document.

Part B

Focus Learner 1

This focus student does not have IEP or learning needs. This student did not have many mistakes on his paper, and he was the one who received the highest score. The learner responds to direct and clear feedback. For the most part, I provided positive feedback to the student to ensure he recognizes that he did well on the assignment. I clearly stated on his rubric sheet that he did a good job in providing details and underlining parts of speech. On the third page, I did make a comment "Did you receive this page?" He made several mistakes that might have been caught if he reviewed his writing. This student did the underlining for the first and second paragraph, so he likely did not review the third or fourth paragraph.

Focus Learner 2

This student has struggled in learning in the past, and this student has to have constant practice to achieve acceptable scores. This is due to him having mild speech disorder and being a struggling reader. As a result, positive feedback is essential for him to process the overall feedback. He also needs suggestions on how to improve scores, so he can apply the suggestion on future assignments. In the rubric, I indicated that to increase the "Content" score he needs to include more details. I provided positive feedback on underlining pronouns and proceeded to indicate that we needed to work on underlining nouns. As mentioned, he has struggled with writing in the past, so I made sure to write a comment on practicing on commas. This student is a visual student, so I made sure to correct all the mistakes on the student's paper. When students failed to underline, I made the correction and circled it. This allowed the student to distinguish that it was an error in underlining and not grammar/spelling/punctuation error.

Focus Learner 3

This learner has difficulty processing visually. To support the student's need, I made sure to use a dark red ink pen. To support the student in spotting his mistakes, I corrected his paper with red ink. Where the student did not underline, I made sure to underline, wrote the part of speech, and made a circle. This will allow the student to process the feedback with little difficulty. On the student's paper, I also made a cloud around any comments I wrote to get the student to read the comment. The student did show good strength in identifying pronouns, and I indicated that as well. In addition, the student also did a good job in underlining verbs, adverbs, and adjectives, and I made sure to document that. The student constantly missed using the article "the", so I provided the student with a comment to read carefully and to proofread.

Part C

I supported the focus students to understand the feedback by directly making corrections on their paper. Moreover, if they failed to underline a word, I made sure to underline and indicate the part of speech, and I also circled the word to ensure students view the correction. If the student constantly made the same mistake, I made sure to comment on that to minimize the chances of it reoccurring in future assignments. For example, focus student 3, failed to use the word "the" when needed. I documented that on his paper. Similarly, focus student 2, failed to include commas when needed, so I wrote on his paper "Remember COMMAS are IMPORTANT." For focus student 3, I wrote on the rubric to "Watch out for spelling!!!" as he had two spelling errors.

Lesson 4 was completed around the end of the week, so students are required to write a reflection in their journal before leaving school. While students completed the journal, I went over the feedback with each student individually. Also, I gave the students opportunity to ask questions regarding the feedback.

The students will be writing essays and paragraphs in future lessons, so the feedback provided to students can be used. Students can use the feedback when they complete journal entries each week. Students are required to write essay a part of end of year summative exam for exiting third grade; this feedback will be helpful in obtaining a good score. Writing is also involved in other academic areas, so the feedback can be applied in multiple settings.

Evidence of Language Understanding and Use

Part A

The students were able to use the language function of writing paragraphs/sentences in the learning experiences. For example, in Clip 1, the student wrote a sentence on the SMART Board (Clip 1, timestamp: 3:23). One of the student struggle to underline one of the nouns in the sentence she wrote (Clip 1, timestamp 3:54).In writing sentences, the students were required to use proper syntax (writing convention).

In lesson four, the students were required to write a short essay. The essay requirements were to use and underline nouns, pronouns, verbs, adverbs, and adjectives. The essay also required the student to use proper writing convention (related skill). As seen in the sample response, some students struggled to underline nouns, verbs, and adverbs. In fact, focus student 2 and focus student 3 made minor mistakes with underlining pronouns. The struggle was not with understanding the vocabulary words (nouns, pronouns, verbs, adverbs, and adjectives), but more with identifying the use of the parts of speech.

Task 3 Part D: Evaluation Criteria

Part A

With most students struggling with identifying nouns, I recommend doing a lesson just focused on nouns and having students complete more hands on activities to apply knowledge.

After that, I recommend the students be introduced to regular nouns, irregular nouns, abstract nouns, regular verbs, and irregular verbs. To connect with prior learning, I can introduce these terms and have the student look at the short essay written in lesson four to see if they already have unknowingly used these parts of speech.

Focus student 1 showed the highest achievement. To challenge the student and continue further development, I think having the student complete advance worksheets of identifying nouns, pronouns, verbs, adverbs, and adjectives to allow him to become more proficient. For focus student 2, I recommend doing a lesson on proper use of commas and have the student complete a writing essay assignment and underlining nouns, pronouns, verbs, adverbs, and adjectives. For focus student 3, I recommend doing an assignment/worksheet on proper use of articles (a, an, and the) in writing.

Part B

As indicated above in the performance analysis and indicated in the students' sample works, the students had most difficulty with underlining nouns. Therefore, to do a re-engagement lesson on nouns is critical to proceed forward in understanding additional types of nouns.

The logical next step instruction is for students to develop knowledge on the types of nouns (regular nouns and irregular nouns) and types of verbs (regular verbs and irregular verbs). This follows a logical sequence and aligns with the sequence of the Common Core standards and builds on prior knowledge. I also recommended using prior work students completed as a way to teach the new concepts. All this is supported by Theorist Jerome Bruner, who state children work best when actively building on their current and past knowledge.

For focus learner 1, having the student do an advance worksheet on identifying nouns, pronouns, verbs, adverbs, and adjectives allows deeper thinking, which is supported by Harvey Daniels, educational researcher and author. Giving students challenging assignments allows them to expand thinking skills, allowing them to become more proficient. Focus learner 2 had the lowest score, and his IEP does mention repetition of work to achieve higher score. The student will benefit from a writing essay assignment and underlining nouns, pronouns, verbs, adverbs, and adjectives based on performance and IEP recommendation. Focus learner 3 recommendation was based on performance of the student as the use of articles (a, an, and the) is important in writing.

Task 3: Part D – Evaluation Criteria

Total Score:

Name: _____   Date of Evaluation:_____

Evaluation Criteria

	Needs Improvement	Acceptable	Good	Outstanding
Content *The student provides an organized, meaningful response to one of the prompts.*	1	2	3	4
Nouns/Pronouns *The student properly uses and underlines nouns/pronouns.*	1	2	3	4
Verbs/Adverbs *The student properly uses and underlines verbs/adverbs.*	1	2	3	4
Adjectives *The student properly uses and underlines adjectives.*	1	2	3	4
Related Skill (Writing Conventions) *The student writes complete sentences by following writing convections. The student writes with accurate use of punctuation and capitalization rules along with spelling correctly.*	1	2	3	4

Scoring: Outstanding (17-20)   Proficient (14-16)   Learning (11-13)   Below Average (0-10)

Comments:

Elementary Education – Literacy Score and Evaluation Analysis

The Elementary Education edTPA® portfolio received a score of 51. With edTPA® being a subjective exam, the score can be in the range of 49-53 depending on the grader. In all States and university programs, this edTPA® portfolio is considered passing (near mastery is some States).

Below is a table that breaks down the scores for each of the rubrics. The rubric numbers are referenced only, so candidates are recommended to refer to the Elementary Education – Literacy handbook for rubric details.

Rubric	Score	Comments/Analysis
1	4	The candidate planned lessons to build on each other with meaningful context. The essential literacy strategy (identifying via underlining parts of speech) for composing text was used in each of the lessons. Throughout the lessons, a consistent connection to related skill existed.
2	4	The instructional tasks were at the right level for the students. The planned supports connect to the students (posters and jeopardy game). Students with specific needs were taken into consideration by using visual aids and large print materials.
3	4	The candidate connected to prior knowledge as the reading articles were grade appropriate. Also, the students have learned the basic writing convection and have been exposed to nouns and pronouns. The reading articles were related to the students' interest (sports and outside environment). The students like to play games, so using a jeopardy game connected to students' interest. The candidates discussed and made connection to research/theories.
4	3	The planned supports indicated in the portfolio were general. To obtain higher score, candidate needed to include more specific planned supports.
5	4	The candidates used multiple informal and formal assessments throughout the lessons. The assessments required essential literacy strategy (writing) and related skills (writing convention).
6	4	Throughout the video, the candidate showed respect and rapport to all students. The candidate also challenged the students to further learning and promoted respect among students.
7	3	The candidate connected prior academic learning to literacy, and the connection to personal assets is general. The students were engaged in tasks that addressed understanding of essential literacy strategy and related skills.
8	3	The candidate provided leading questions to elicit response. Repetition is also used to get the students to respond. Taking turn approach engages the students to participate. As the candidates elicit response, the students were involved in the essential literacy strategy.
9	3	The candidate explicitly showed the essential literacy strategy to the students. Many opportunities existed for the student to practice the essential literacy strategy.
10	4	Candidate included the changes and reasons for the changes. Justification was

		connected to students' performance and research/theory.
11	4	The candidate used examples from work samples to explain patterns of learning (all students performing well on pronouns). The candidate also explained in detail patterns of learning for the whole class.
12	3	The feedback provided was more focused on the strength than needs. The feedback was related to the objectives.
13	2	Feedback was provided to the students, but opportunities did not exist that allowed the learners to use feedback. To increase the score, the candidate could provide more opportunities to apply feedback and support the students in using the feedback. Information provided was general.
14	3	The candidate does an acceptable job explaining the use of language function and language demands. The candidate reference evidence for video and sample work.
15	3	The next steps of instruction were general. The connection to research and theory was also general. The next step of instruction was more related to the objectives of the lessons.
Total Score	51	This edTPA® portfolio is considered passing (near mastery level). The lesson plans were related to an appropriate essential strategy (underlining/identifying) for third grade level. The use of related skill was widely used in lesson plans. Assessments provided tested the students' knowledge on objectives, essential strategy, and related skill. The candidate used various materials and instructional methods targeted English learners and students with learning needs. Commentary responses were well written (with a few exceptions).

This page is intentionally left blank.

Chapter 16 – Lesson Plan Template

Many candidates are confused about what information to include in the lesson plans for edTPA®. Below is a lesson plan template that can be used for any edTPA® portfolio. This is a general outline where the candidates can fill in the necessary information.

Lesson Title/Grade Level

Central Focus (or Learning Goal)

Educational Standards

Lesson Objectives (Only document objectives that are going to be measured)

Instructional Material/Resources

Identification of Students Prerequisite Knowledge and Skills

Instructional Procedures (step by step instructional procedures)

Closure Procedures (Explain how the lesson is going to be closed)

Guided Practice/Independent Practice/Planned Supports/Communication Skill

Differentiated Instruction (Describe in bullet points how you differentiated instruction to accommodate English learners, learning needs students, and/or general education students.)

Assessments (Describe in bullet points formal/informal

This page is intentionally left blank.